LEADING
LEARNING

ROSEMARYE T. TAYLOR

LEADING LEARNING

Change

Student

Achievement

Today!

CORWIN
A SAGE Company

For information:

Corwin
A SAGE Company
2455 Teller Road
Thousand Oaks, California 91320
(800) 233-9936
Fax: (800) 417-2466
www.corwinpress.com

SAGE Ltd.
1 Oliver's Yard
55 City Road
London EC1Y 1SP
United Kingdom

SAGE India Pvt. Ltd.
B 1/I 1 Mohan Cooperative
   Industrial Area
Mathura Road, New Delhi 110 044
India

SAGE Asia-Pacific Pte. Ltd.
33 Pekin Street #02-01
Far East Square
Singapore 048763

Printed in the United States of America.

Library of Congress Cataloging-in-Publication Data

Taylor, Rosemarye, 1950-
Leading learning: change student achievement today!/Rosemarye T. Taylor.
      p. cm.
Includes bibliographical references and index.
ISBN 978-1-4129-7870-5 (pbk.)
   1. School improvement programs. 2. Academic achievement. 3. Educational leadership. I. Title.

LB2822.8.T39 2010
371.2'07—dc22   2009026776

This book is printed on acid-free paper.

09   10   11   12   13   10   9   8   7   6   5   4   3   2   1

Acquisitions Editor:	Arnis Burvikovs
Associate Editor:	Desirée A. Bartlett
Editorial Assistant:	Joanna Coelho
Production Editor:	Eric Garner
Copy Editor:	Gretchen Treadwell
Typesetter:	C&M Digitals (P) Ltd.
Proofreader:	Joyce Li
Indexer:	Kathleen Paparchontis
Cover Designer:	Karine Hovsepian

Contents

List of Tables

List of Resources

Preface

Leaders are held accountable for gains in student achievement through various measures, particularly state-identified assessments. Nationally, the No Child Left Behind Act of 2001 (NCLB) requires that students read on grade level by 2014. *The Nation's Report Card: Reading 2007* (Lee, Grigg, & Donahue, 2007) shows that although students are making progress in reading on the National Assessment of Educational Progress (NAEP), it is slight. In reading, 67 percent of fourth graders performed at the basic level and 33 percent at the proficient level in 2007. Reading performance is similar at the eighth-grade level with 74 percent performing at the basic level and 31 percent at the proficient level. Perhaps more importantly, there remains a gap between the learning of African-American and Hispanic students and their white counterparts. It is not surprising that the same holds true for students living in poverty and those who are not. Nationally, the goal is for more students to perform at the proficient level on a nationally accepted assessment, such as NAEP, since the state assessments vary in where proficiency is set—below, at, or above grade level. To further address this goal, *Leading Learning: Change Student Achievement Today!* provides leader actions and examples where the gap in learning is closing through exceptional leadership.

Many leaders are seeking perfect solutions to this challenge in the form of instructional resources. As leaders at both the district and school levels consider steps to make these changes, they often find that only small improvements can be made with new resources alone and without implementing significant changes. These dramatic changes result in rethinking organization, roles of individuals, and how learning is approached; these are called *second-order changes*. Second-order change often makes people feel uncomfortable because it represents a departure from accepted practice in that district or school and means new learning for those involved.

Marzano, Waters, and McNulty (2005) distinguish between first-order change and second-order change by identifying first-order change as incremental and gradual, and seen as the logical next step for a school or district. Second-order change is dramatic in both how the problem is defined and how the solution is approached. Second-order change is deep change that alters the system in fundamental ways, offering a dramatic shift in direction and requiring new ways of thinking and acting (p. 66).

Because of the need to improve achievement for all students and the accountability faced by leaders searching for solutions, I began examining what successful leaders do who lead second-order change. After a number of years as a school administrator, district administrator, and now university faculty member and consultant, I have spent many days in classrooms, schools, and districts seeking to find the perfect solution for making gains in student achievement. This interest led to researching what leaders who make significant change in schools do to make such gains in student achievement. After interviewing sixty-two leaders (fifty school principals and twelve district leaders), studying their data, and visiting their schools and districts, I found that there is no one best solution to improve learning for all students, but there are patterns and themes inherent in what leaders today do to have positive results. I call these patterns "leader action themes for second-order change" (see Table 1.4) and they are shared throughout the book in the context of the school or district setting.

The key finding is that leaders change the culture of the school or district to focus on all students learning at a higher level. Keep in mind that, for some, the mantra of all students learning at a higher level is second-order change, resulting in altered professional practice. This requires significant rethinking about leadership, teaching, and learning and is a departure from previous practice. For example, shared in this text, teachers in these settings are now expected to collaborate when they previously worked in isolation. Aligned with the expectation for teachers to collaborate is for leadership to hold teachers accountable for that collaboration and resulting change in student achievement. Prior to this change, teachers may have been independent in their curriculum implementation, instruction, assessment, or use of resources, but the second-order change is to align the curriculum and resource implementation. Another example, also included in this book, is the change in attitude that results in teaching more diverse students in high-level classes. This replaces the attitude of exclusion except for only a few selected students. These examples require different thinking about one's work and the results expected from the work.

To accomplish these substantive changes, leaders begin with data study and sharing of that data with other administrators and teachers. Together, they come to conclusions drawing from their knowledge of the daily practice in the district or school. Following the contextualized data study, steps are determined for leading the enhancement of knowledge and skill, followed by daily practice related to the target change. Accountability for making the target changes is ever present. Strategic data study by all participants is ongoing to monitor implementation and to adjust decisions related to the target change. All decisions focus on the learning needs of the students.

WHO WILL BENEFIT FROM THIS BOOK?

Since this book is based on actions that leaders believe influenced positive changes in student achievement in their schools and districts, practitioners and those interested in changing learning should find the ideas useful. District leaders who are responsible for improving learning will find examples in each chapter. Those who have school-level responsibilities will find examples for elementary, middle, and high schools. Examples are also included representing rural, suburban, and urban contexts. Demographic information is provided to assist the reader in relating to each example: keep in mind that many suburban districts have characteristics typically attributed to urban districts, indicating demographic change in some suburban communities.

This book may also be helpful for leadership teams, including teacher leaders and community leaders, as they consider steps to build support for making changes that may create some uneasiness. What readers may find interesting is that while the context and players in each chapter change, the leader actions remain consistent.

HOW IS THE BOOK ORGANIZED?

Each chapter of *Leading Learning: Change Student Achievement Today!* begins with a brief presentation of the research theme exemplified within. The theme discussions are followed with practical examples and insights provided by school and district leaders. These individuals represent varying levels of students and various demographic settings—from rural to urban and from high poverty to economically advantaged. Some of the examples are from my own experience working in districts and schools; therefore, the example may not be from an interview in the identified research. Because each of these leaders exemplifies at least eight of the themes, the scenarios include more than one theme to give the reader the context for the change, but are selected for a chapter as the best example for that particular theme.

A reflection on the theme is used to summarize key points. Next are a few practical tips for implementation. Following the practical tips, trends related to the chapter's theme serve as a quick reference. Each chapter then concludes with helpful terms. Within the Resources, the reader will find artifacts associated with the changes in these schools and districts which principals thought may be helpful in replication of a specific change.

Chapter 9 emerged as the ninth theme from the research through examples provided during the discussions. Most of those interviewed indicate that politics, as the participants interpreted the word, were not an issue and that school boards are supportive of the second-order changes. However, in my reflections, it has become clear that while most interviewees say that politics are not an issue, their leader actions are political, or they leverage their position to influence second-order change, or, because of their unique position, influence second-order change differently.

The last chapter, "Reflections on Leading Learning for Second-Order Change," provides a summary of the components of the second-order changes such as curriculum, instruction, and assessment. These components are trends of the target changes observed in the schools and districts making gains in student achievement. These components are represented in the outer band of Table 1.3.

WHAT ARE THE SPECIAL FEATURES?

Because of the pressure on leaders to make improvements in student achievement and the accountability for doing so, there are numerous publications on the topic. What makes this book unique is that while it is based on research, it represents leaders *now*, dedicated to improving learning for all students. It is not a historical or theoretical perspective, but one of timely, real examples, which may provide guidance to those seeking to lead change. Furthermore, the examples are presented in context and it is noted that to make these successful changes, difficulties may arise, but can be facilitated with these leader action themes.

The organization of the book is unique and should be a helpful resource.

- Introduction of leader action theme
- Real examples in varying contexts
- Reflection summary
- Practical tips
- Summary of trends
- Helpful terms
- Tables showing data and examples
- Figures to create a mental model of change in learning
- Resources provided by schools

REFLECTION

Leading learning to improve achievement for all students requires deeper and different thinking than in previous years. Teachers and leaders cannot just do what they have been doing better. Educators have to think differently, do different things, and do them consistently well. Leaders must reconceptualize their role and the role of each of their faculty, staff, and administration to optimize success related to all students learning at higher levels.

Acknowledgments

Leaders who participated in the school and district visits and interviews were willing to share what they learned and what they attributed the successful implementation of second-order change. My thanks go to these individuals for their courageous leadership, commitment to all students, and commitment to the profession by sharing their journeys of second-order change with me, and now with you. Also, the study would not have taken place without the thoughtful recommendations from colleagues and leaders for who should be included.

Particular appreciation is extended to those leaders who are described in leader action themes, in the leader in action scenarios in this book, and those who agreed to be interviewed.

Jada Askew
Mike Blasewitz
Patty Bowen-Painter
Harold Border
Carol Chanter
Kate Clark
Connie Collins
Tim Cool
Anna Marie Cote
Tom Curry
Cynthia Dodge
Bill Farrell
Donald Fennoy
Raymond Gaines
Larry Gerardot
Pete Gorman
Walt Griffin
Fred Heid
Janet Hurt

Barbara Jenkins
Carol Kelley
James Kusmaul
Gonzalo La Cava
Mark McCoy
Van Mitchell
Dale Moxley
Barrett Nelson
Beverly Perrault
Janie Phelps
Les Potter
Jaime Quinones
Grant Rivera
David Roland
Linda Romans
Paul Sansom
Nancy Simon
Patrick Simon
Thomas Smith

Paula St. Francis   Bill Vogel
Pam Tapley   Cindy Westover
Joy Taylor   Ken Winn
Todd Trimble   John Wright

Without the assistance from Elaina LeGros, graduate assistant, the data search would have delayed the publication. She searched, for many hours, for school and district data supporting that the second-order changes resulted in gains in student achievement.

About the Author

**Rosemarye (Rose) T. Taylor** has a rich background that includes middle and high school teaching and school administration. She was a reading, language arts, and Spanish teacher, followed by service as a middle and high school administrator, and district-level administrator in Georgia and Florida. In private sector management, she was director of professional development for Scholastic, Inc., New York. Currently, she is associate professor of educational leadership at the University of Central Florida in Orlando.

Much of her success is due to conceptualizing, creating, and implementing fail-safe systems that work seamlessly to support improvements in student learning. As an example, Taylor led research, design, and implementation of the Orange County Literacy Program that has successfully impacted thousands of elementary, middle, and high school students and teachers. The classroom concept designed, implemented, and evaluated with her leadership has been produced as a literacy intervention product by Scholastic, Inc. Additionally, in Orange County Public Schools, Orlando, Florida, she designed and implemented a curriculum system including curriculum, instruction, assessment, and professional development supporting the notion that systems make the work of administrators and teachers easier. A consistent thread in these successful systems is supporting the development and implementation of learning communities to advance student achievement. This occurs by providing structure within which to empower the classroom teachers to make gains day by day.

As associate professor of educational leadership at the University of Central Florida, her specialty is leadership to improve student achievement. She has conducted research on leadership and change, particularly as it relates to accountability. Presentations on this topic have been given at

University Council of Educational Administration, American Association of Educational Research, American Association of School Administrators, National Council of Professors of Educational Administration, Southern Regional Council of Educational Administration, International Reading Association, Association for Supervision and Curriculum Development, National Association of Secondary School Principals, National Association of Elementary Principals, and National Middle School Association conferences. Her articles have been published in *Kappan, Educational Leadership, Middle School Journal, Schools in the Middle, American Secondary Education, AASA Professor, The National Staff Development Journal, Principal Leadership, The School Administrator, Journal of Scholarship and Practice, Educational Research Service Spectrum,* and *International Journal of Education Management.* In addition to this book, she has authored *Improving Reading, Writing, and Content Learning for Students in Grades 4–12* (2007), *Leadership Handbook for Literacy Coaching* (2006), *The K–12 Literacy Leadership Fieldbook* (2005), *Literacy Leadership for Grades 5–12,* (2003), and *Leading With Character to Improve Student Achievement* (2003). She serves as consultant on improving student achievement through literacy, learning communities, curriculum system development, and leadership to schools, districts, and professional organizations.

1

Introduction and Background

This chapter will present the research supporting the content of the following chapters. The genesis for the research is the interest in improving learning for all students and how leaders who are successful in doing so make these improvements. Because of the accountability felt by school and district leaders today, many are not able to achieve their target improvements with small, incremental changes (first-order changes); they instead expect changes that require different actions, attitudes, and skills of everyone involved in schools. These changes—impacting how learning takes place and, perhaps, how it is measured—are referred to as second-order changes. Second-order changes are the focus of the research supporting the content in this book.

HOW DID THE RESEARCH BEGIN?

To quantify the themes encountered in my experience as a school and district administrator and consultant in schools, I began with the meta-analysis based works of Marzano, Waters, and McNulty (2005) and Waters and Marzano (2007). These studies identify leadership factors of second-order change related to gains in student achievement at the school and district level, respectively. From a rigorous review of research on principal leadership and student-achievement studies published from 1978–2001, Marzano, Waters, and McNulty (2005) found about 5,000 studies, but only sixty-nine met the criteria sought for the meta-analysis. In the meta-analysis of these studies, the authors identified twenty-one factors of leadership. Of those, seven factors seem to be related to second-order change, or change that is deep, and that requires rethinking pedagogy or delivery of educational services. Marzano, Waters, and McNulty's seven factors, in order of importance, are:

1. Knowledge of curriculum, instruction, and assessment.
2. Optimizer.
3. Intellectual stimulation.
4. Change agent.
5. Monitoring/evaluating.
6. Flexibility.
7. Ideals/beliefs (p. 70).

Similar to the review and meta-analysis of studies on principal leadership, Waters and Marzano (2007) reviewed more than 4,500 titles and found twenty-seven that met the required criteria for inclusion in a study of district leadership impacting student achievement. In the meta-analysis of the studies on district leadership and student achievement, five factors were found to have a positive correlation to student achievement. These are, in this order:

1. Collaborative goal-setting process.
2. Nonnegotiable goals for achievement and instruction.
3. Board alignment with and support of district goals.
4. Monitoring the goals for achievement and instruction.
5. Use of resources to support the goals for achievement and instruction (p. 3).

Table 1.2 illustrates the relationship of district and school leadership factors.

WHY INTERVIEW RESEARCH?

For those who read and discuss research, the value of different methodologies inevitably comes into question. Is the meta-analysis conclusive enough for school leaders to focus on those identified factors in implementing innovation? Furthermore, many of the studies in the cited research took place in schools and districts that were radically different than the context in which schools and districts find themselves today. This reflection led me to embark on interview research with sixty-two school principals and district leaders who were identified by other leaders as having successfully implemented second-order change. Another twenty-three leaders were recommended, but twenty-one of those did not have student-achievement data supporting the successful second-order change; therefore, I chose to not extend the invitation to be interviewed. Two others did not desire to participate in the study.

In the interview protocols (Resources A and B), most of the interview items are directly related to the factors identified by Marzano, Waters, and McNulty (2005) for the principal interview and Waters and Marzano (2007) for the district-leader interview. There is also an item on each interview protocol related to changes made to the structure, organization, professional development, and use of resources. This item was derived from experience as a school and district leader, observations of improved schools, and literature (Bolman & Deal, 2003; Leithwood, Louis, Anderson & Wahlstrom, 2004; Taylor & Collins, 2003). Generally, I did not have to ask each of the questions, since the leaders addressed the target content within the discussions. They were anxious to share what they had done and the resulting successes related to teacher and student accomplishments.

In all but two principal and one district leader interviews, I spent time in each school or district, either before or after the interview, becoming knowledgeable of the context and implementation of the second-order change. In all cases, student-achievement data was gathered to support the successful implementation of second-order change before the interview. Often, the leader provided additional data during the visit.

WHO PARTICIPATED IN THE INTERVIEWS?

Fifty principals and twelve district leaders, in ten states, were interviewed between October 2007 and April 2009. Thirty-three of the principals interviewed were in their first assignment as principal and twelve were in their second assignment as principal. These numbers may counter the thinking that the more experience principals have, the more expert they will be at leading change. Rather than experience, perhaps decision makers should ask, "What attitude, skills, and knowledge do leaders need to lead significant change in schools and districts?"

All but one district leader was a principal before moving into district-level leadership. Interestingly, these district leaders indicate that their leadership philosophies and practices have not changed from when they were principals. What did change is their expanded views and scope of responsibility, but their actions to bring about change, identified in this text as leader action themes, did not change. This commonality in the leaders' practices, whether serving at the school or district levels, is why the leader action themes are the same for leaders working at both levels.

Table 1.1 provides more information about the participants. There were slightly more males than females, mostly at the secondary level. The majority of district leaders in the research were female. Most of the participants were white. A point of note is that one half of the participants either had earned a doctorate degree or were in a doctoral program at the time of the interview.

Table 1.1   Demographic Variables of Participants

Position	Gender		Race			Doctorate		
	Male	Female	White	Hispanic	African American	Yes	In Program	No
Elementary Principals N = 16	4	12	14	1	1	6	2	8
Middle School Principals N = 12	10	2	12	0	0	4	2	6
K–8 Principals N = 2	2	0	2	0	0	0	0	2
High School Principals N = 20	15	5	14	2	4	8	4	8
District Leaders N = 12	3	9	10	0	2	5	0	7
Total N = 62	34	28	52	3	7	23	8	31

WHAT ACTIONS DO THESE LEADERS TAKE?

Interview research from 2007–2009 indicates that these leaders employ the factors of second-order change identified by Marzano, Waters, and McNulty (2005) and Waters and Marzano (2007). The findings also reflect a mosaic of the recent work of Blase and Blase (2001, 2004); Reeves (2006); Wagner and Kagan (2006); Fullan (2006); DuFour (2004); and Leithwood, Louis, Anderson, and Walhstrom (2004). Content and themes of the leader responses do not have great variation, regardless of the level of the students served, demographics of the students, geographic location, characteristics of the community, nor personal characteristics or position of the leader—either at the school or district. *All students learning is the consistent priority across every interview and visit, and everything else is less important.*

Themes that emerged from the research are more precise than factors (see Table 1.2) identified by Marzano, Waters, and McNulty (2005) and Waters and Marzano (2007), reflecting the accountability faced by leaders in 2009 and the leaders' knowledge of contemporary research. As mentioned, the responses of both district leaders and principals are similar; therefore, I combined them into the nine leader action themes for second-order change. The intent is to show what actions the leaders perceive result in improved student achievement in their schools and districts.

Table 1.2 Relationship of Factors of Second-Order Change: District and School-Based Leadership

School-Based Leadership	District Leadership
Knowledge of Curriculum, Instruction, Assessment	Nonnegotiable Goals for Achievement and Instruction
Optimizer	Use of Resources to Support Goals for Achievement and Instruction
Intellectual Stimulation	Collaborative Goal Setting
Change Agent	Use of Resources to Support Goals for Achievement and Instruction
Monitoring and Evaluating	Monitoring of Goals for Achievement and Instruction
Flexibility	
Ideals and Beliefs	Nonnegotiable Goals for Achievement and Instruction
	Board Alignment With and Support of District Goals for Achievement and Instruction

Source: Marzano, Waters, & McNulty (2005)

Source: Waters & Marzano (2007)

One hundred percent of those interviewed identified the first seven themes as related to their second-order change. Many of the principals identified family and community engagement to be important to their students' improved learning. The ninth theme emerged within each of the discussions.

These themes are not listed in order of importance, but it appears that to change a culture to one focused on learning, a leader would have to take action on most of the remaining themes. Therefore, focusing the school or district culture on learning is the central concept of this text. The reader can see from Table 1.3 that it is in the center, and the other surrounding themes

Table 1.3   Leading Learning for Second-Order Change: Conceptual Model

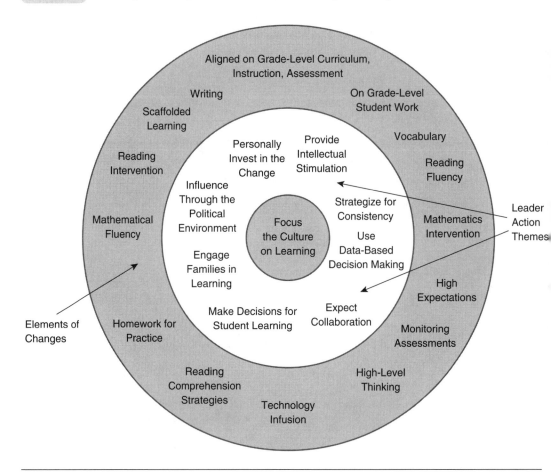

support the culture on learning. The nine leader action themes for second-order change are:

1. Leaders focus the culture on learning.
2. Leaders make decisions for student learning.
3. Leaders stimulate intellectual growth.
4. Leaders invest personally in the change.
5. Leaders expect collaboration to optimize success.
6. Leaders strategize for consistency.
7. Leaders provide the expectation and support for data-based decision making.
8. Leaders engage families in learning.
9. Leaders influence through the political environment.

The fact that leaders believe that changing the culture to focus on learning is significant tells us that it was not focused this way before they assumed the leadership position. If leaders focus the culture on learning, and if that is second-order change, how do they accomplish this culture change? The eight other leader action themes support changing the school or district culture to one focused on all students learning. These themes do not appear to take place in any order, but common sense tells us that that making decisions for student learning is a precursor that guides other leader action themes. Intellectual stimulation probably precedes the expectations of other actions.

Table 1.4 shows each theme and examples of leader actions. This table may be a helpful quick reference as each chapter is read or as a resource for collaboration with others. To what extent are these leader action themes present in your setting? What steps can be taken to implement those that you think will enhance student achievement?

Table 1.4   Leader Action Themes for Second-Order Change

Themes	Examples From Interviews
1. *Leaders focus the culture of the school or district on learning.*	✓ Culture is focused on learning. ✓ High expectations are demonstrated for all (ESE, ESL, average, gifted) in curriculum, instruction, and student work. ✓ A philosophy of inclusion is adopted in advanced classes, rather than exclusion/elitism. ✓ Focus is on student and adult relationships. ✓ Discussions are opened on the concepts that reflect learning, such as grading practices.
2. *Leaders make decisions for student learning.*	✓ Districts and schools are reorganized for effective and efficient use of time, people, space, and resources. ✓ Teams of teachers and/or administrators are strategically revised to leverage expertise, knowledge, and attitudes. ✓ Physical location of teachers is adjusted to facilitate collaboration. ✓ Teacher leadership teams are changed from department or grade-level chairs to collaborative team leaders.

(Continued)

Table 1.4 (Continued)

Themes	Examples From Interviews
	✓ Use of time within and beyond the school day is rearranged for student results—before-school and afterschool care, tutoring, detention, and supervision time become targeted instructional time. ✓ Teachers/administrators/support staff self-select to leave, are reassigned, or are nonrenewed.
3. *Leaders stimulate intellectual growth.*	✓ Leaders easily talk about research. ✓ Leaders attend professional development and conferences with teacher teams. ✓ Accountability for results is supported with professional development. ✓ Study groups/book studies/action research focus on the target need and are led by principals, administrators, and teachers. ✓ In-house experts provide collaborative support for colleagues. ✓ Professional development evolves from workshops to voluntary study/action research teams, book studies, collegial class visits, etc. ✓ Curriculum, instruction, and assessment are studied.
4. *Leaders personally invest in second-order change and are involved.*	✓ Leaders do not delegate student achievement. ✓ Leaders attend the professional development/professional learning community sessions/data study with administrators and teachers. ✓ Leaders visit classrooms regularly and provide feedback. ✓ Leaders have authentic conversations with subordinates about student learning and subordinate performance.
5. *Leaders expect collaboration and results from collaboration.*	✓ Leaders lead changes with the nonnegotiable of collaboration. ✓ Leaders use collaboration to support change. ✓ Leaders collaborate with one another. ✓ Leaders seek divergent thinking and feedback. ✓ Teacher teams are expected to collaborate and to provide evidence/artifacts of results. ✓ Each year, accountability for collaborating to achieve results increases.

Themes	Examples From Interviews
6. *Leaders strategize for consistency to ensure that the leadership team speaks with the same voice.*	✓ Leaders create an expectation of consistency through personal, active participation. ✓ Leaders are purposeful and deliberate in implementing systems and structures to ensure consistency. ✓ Leaders meet regularly with subordinate leaders to prepare them to speak with the same voice and to have a level of knowledge and skills necessary to provide consistent expectations. ✓ Leaders meet regularly with teacher leaders to clarify misconceptions and focus the work. ✓ Leaders regularly visit classrooms.
7. *Leaders provide the expectation and support for data-based decision making at the teacher level.*	✓ Student data is used to drive budget decisions. ✓ Accountability for results is clear. ✓ Online instructional plans—requiring literacy strategies, high levels of questioning, and attention to individual students—are monitored. ✓ Follow-up with individual teacher conferences takes place. ✓ Data meetings with teacher teams are held regularly with feedback on steps taken to improve learning. ✓ Various forms of data are used for decision making.
8. *Leaders engage families in the learning process.*	✓ Parents participate in learning about how to ask about school, about assignments, etc. ✓ School offers adult English classes for parents. ✓ Parents learn the instructional philosophy. ✓ Teachers call parents to invite them to events. ✓ Technology is used to provide access for families.
9. *Leaders influence through the political environment.*	✓ Leaders are transparent, public, and accountable about data, purpose, and results. ✓ Leaders develop trust and respectful relationships. ✓ Leveraging political environments is internal and external.

REFLECTION

Leading change in learning is very difficult. There are many who believe that the task of improving learning for all students is overwhelming, and perhaps even impossible. By considering the leader action themes, the work to be done can be conceptualized in manageable units. Consider which leader actions are already in place or progressing. Which ones should you consider next? Perhaps steps have been taken related to particular leader actions, but the accountability or follow-through is not present. Maybe the leader needs encouragement to weather the discomfort that second-order change causes. Based on this research and years of experience, it is my belief that leaders who strategize to improve learning and implement the leader action themes will be successful. The option of only making incremental changes is not viable given accountability for student learning.

HELPFUL TERMS

Correlation: Statistical term that refers to a substantiated relationship between two or more variables.

Meta-analysis: Techniques for statistically forming generalizations across a number of studies.

Second-order change: Deep change that alters the system in fundamental ways, offering a dramatic shift in direction and requiring new ways of thinking and acting (Marzano, Waters, & McNulty, 2005).

2

Focus the Culture on Learning

Make Decisions for Student Learning

Although we know that the purpose of schooling is student learning, when the door is closed and educators speak freely, many admit that some schools are organized for other reasons, primarily adult convenience. Examples of adult convenience include who teaches what, how students are assessed, instructional resources, when planning periods take place, how adults are teamed, and which students a teacher may teach. In contrast, successful leaders in second-order change focus decision making on what is best for each student's achievement. According to those interviewed, this guidance for decision making is evidenced by the culture of the district or school and the organizational structures put into place to maximize all students' learning. This chapter addresses the first two leadership themes: (1) focus the culture of the school or district on learning and (2) make decisions for student learning. It seems that the successful change efforts depend on the leader focusing the culture on learning and making decisions targeting that intended result. The other action themes assist in creating successful learning cultures.

At the initiation of the interviews, I invited the leader to share information related to the innovation surrounding the interview's focus, expecting that he or she would believe that one particular innovation made the difference: "Describe the innovation and the role you played in the design, implementation, and evaluation." Initially, I was surprised that the innovation most often cited was that the culture of the district or school had to be changed. Culture means, "how we do things around here," the behavioral norms the adults and students, and the unwritten rules and rituals representing the values, traditions, language, and expectations for learning (Peterson & Deal, 2002). As an example, Grant Rivera, principal at South Cobb High School, shared, "We suffered from a culture of low expectations." In other words, Grant and other leaders found that the culture was not focused on all students learning at a high level. For instance, it was accepted that some students would not read or write well or be successful in higher levels of mathematics. Consequently, many students experienced levels of curriculum, instruction, and work at levels too low to be successful on state accountability measures.

Learning was not the number one priority as other important issues or tasks took attention. Discipline and safety might have been consuming most of the leaders' time, or dealing with unhappy parents. Furthermore, there were beliefs, norms of behavior, and traditions that reinforced a culture of acceptance of the status quo of student achievement. Peterson (2002) indicates, "When a school has a positive, professional culture, one finds meaningful staff development, successful curricular reform, and the effective use of student performance data" (p. 10). Each of these components was examined in the research, and will be addressed in changing the culture of the schools—resulting in higher student achievement.

To change the culture of the school or district, structures and organization (Bolman & Deal, 2002) changed to facilitate development of a culture resulting in gains in student learning. Similarly, Leithwood, Louis, Anderson, and Wahlstrom (2004) found that schools and districts implementing such changes redesign the cultures and organizational structures while building collaborative processes. Collaborative processes and examples will be discussed more in depth in Chapter 5. Although one principal was told, by a legendary administrator, not to even move a trash can the first year, he encountered a situation that he believed needed immediate adjustments for the sake of the students. This principal said it well: "The school was dysfunctional when I arrived; I reorganized the school and put into place processes that would work and improve learning." Thus, he contributed to changing the culture. Principals and other leaders should not be afraid to make change when it is in the best interest of student learning.

> One novice principal indicated a twenty-year assistant principal was no longer healthy and up to the physically active role of the position. She had difficult discussions about what the job entailed, what she expected, and asked him what he thought he could do to meet the expectations. The assistant principal had never been questioned about his performance or expectations. As a result, he made significant improvements in his contribution to student welfare and learning until he could retire.

Most of the leaders interviewed indicated that with increased accountability for results on their shoulders, they increase accountability for results for faculty, staff, and other administrators. Difficult conversations take place to be sure that everyone knows what is going well and what improvements have to take place. No employee is allowed to be a placeholder—each has to perform at a high level to maximize student learning.

Mike Schmoker (as cited in Reeves, 2006), aptly represents what each leader said that he or she did, causing improvement in performance, or the employee's self-selection to work elsewhere, or nonreappointment. He states, "I'll ask the uncomfortable questions, make sure certain things are happening, and confront people not doing them" (p. 3). What is interesting is that of those nonrenewed or career counseled out of a particular position, few of these leaders were contacted for references before the former employee was hired to work in another educational setting. Each position counts just as each student counts, so seeking authentic references on potential employees is essential to improve learning.

Following are scenarios of leaders in various locations serving all levels of students. To change the culture to one focused on all students learning, decisions are made in the best interest of students.

LEADER IN ACTION

Paula St. Francis, Rimfire Elementary School

I had to create a culture of learning.

—Paula St. Francis

Rimfire Elementary School: Rural		
Students: 1,346 Teachers: 93		
Poverty: 57%		
ELL: 10%	ESE: 22%	
White: 59%	African American: 17%	Hispanic: 12%
Multiracial: 9% Asian: 3%		

Paula St. Francis opened Rimfire Elementary School in 2006 in a community transitioning from rural to suburban, with 60 percent of the faculty having less than five years of teaching experience. Due to the lack of teaching experience, Paula saw her task was to create a culture of learning by creating clear expectations for the teachers and targeted professional development. This would place the teachers in a process of continual professional growth. Now, every decision at Rimfire is data based so that objectivity reigns over professional folktales or prior professional practice; data eliminates the emotionality in the decision making for student learning.

Students at Rimfire have a mobility rate of 38 percent, meaning that many of the students who start the school year at Rimfire are somewhere else by the end of the school year. With the demographics in the sidebar, one can see that the school is a mix of students with varying academic needs requiring teachers with expertise in serving diverse learners.

The first thing Paula identified to do was develop a high level of trust in the relationships among teachers and administrators. With a high level of trust, they would be more likely to implement the innovations that she envisioned. This was important since the focus was on building the professional skills of novice teachers while enhancing learning for all of the diverse learners. To build trust, she listened, listened, and listened some more to the faculty and staff. She committed to being in every class a minimum of twice each week to support and provide high-quality feedback, and to monitor instruction. Every day, the leadership team ate lunch together for purposeful and meaningful conversation on what each had observed in classrooms and throughout the school that day—developing patterns, and interventions needed.

Organizationally, the school needed a structure to support the development of each teacher and the attention to individual student data-based needs. Teachers were organized in small learning communities (SLCs) by grade level in 2006. These groups were large and some teachers were not as involved as others. By the third year, SLCs were reorganized to be no more than six teachers with strategic groupings based on teacher skill and need.

The expectation is that the discussions within the small learning communities focus on student learning. Teachers develop common assessments that serve to drive instruction, pacing, and reteaching when necessary. The physical locations of teachers have been moved to strategically place those who can provide needed expertise close to others who may benefit from it, and also to encourage collaboration.

This physical reorganization of the school relates to the strategic focus on developing the professional skill of the less experienced teachers as well as those with more experience. In addition to the expectation of collaborative learning, professional development is ongoing. Professional development takes place in the school and often by the teachers themselves. They have action research projects and book studies on vocabulary development, fluency development, and asking higher-order questions to encourage teachers' own growth and sharing.

One of the most effective professional development experiences at Rimfire has been professional data days. On these days, teachers bring their student data and student work to share with each other. Paula is fond of saying, "Look to your left, look to your right. Ask a question that will help you with your data and student learning. Is there someone you want to learn from?" This strategy sets up the expectation to learn from one another and to support each other with one's own expertise. No teacher is alone. Resource C includes the guidelines used by Rimfire for collaboration.

Paula has created a culture of learning at Rimfire Elementary School. In the fall of 2009, the school added middle grades to the K–5 already present.

Parents, teachers, and the community are happy with the school that has been created and graded as an A school by the Florida Department of Education for its first two years. In the 2008 school year, there were sixty-five applications for the one teacher vacancy at the school, indicating that the culture of learning attracts professionals, and not just students.

LEADER IN ACTION

Les Potter, Silver Sands Middle School

We do not allow students to fail.

—Les Potter

Silver Sands Middle School: Suburban		
Students: 1,273	Teachers: 68	
Poverty: 20%	ELL: 2%	ESE: 22%
White: 87%	African American: 10%	Hispanic: 2%

Les Potter has been principal of Silver Sands Middle School for eight years. During this tenure, the focus has been on building a positive culture for learning and for students. His philosophy is simple, "Is it good for kids and learning?" That simple question guides decision making and keeps everyone focused on the purpose of the school. To that end, decisions and the organization of the school are guided.

An example of his philosophy is that all teachers have forty-five minutes of duty-free lunch. Within that time, they often volunteer to tutor students who need extra help. They have learned that students do not like to stay after school for assistance or may not have transportation home so tutoring at lunch is mandatory for students who need intervention. Teacher participation is voluntary. Because the culture is focused on all students being successful, Les encounters little resistance from faculty. This solution of lunchtime tutoring was developed by the behavior leadership team, a team of teachers at the school who develop solutions to schoolwide issues and submit them to the administration for consideration.

Another seemingly controversial practice relates to grading. When Les studied research on grading, he concluded that many of the accepted practices are not in the best interest of all students. At Silver Sands Middle School, the lowest grade that can be given for homework is 50 percent. This way, if a student does not complete homework or does not have a home life that supports homework completion, the student can still make a passing grade if the work is completed within the school day and is of quality as judged by the teacher.

How does Les know that the culture for learning is working? Student referrals to the administrators for misbehavior are down 50 percent from when Les arrived at the school. In 2007, only two eighth-grade students were not promoted to the high school. Teacher turnover is minimal since those who leave do so for retirement rather than to move to another school. Silver Sands Middle School is consistently graded an A by the Department of Education in Florida.

Osceola High School: Urban

Students: 1,640   Teachers: 90

Poverty: 21%   ELL: 12%   ESE: 15%

White: 83%   African   Hispanic: 5%
                American: 6%

Asian: 3%   Multiracial: 3%

LEADER IN ACTION

Carol Moore, Osceola High School

> *Carol changed the culture of our school!*

—Teacher

When visiting Osceola High School, Carol Moore extended an open invitation to faculty to meet and share with me what has taken place over the previous four years. The group who voluntarily met after school was emphatic about Carol's leadership, represented by the quote above. First of all, it is unusual for teachers to talk about the culture of the school using that language, rather than pointing out specific kinds of changes they experienced. Having a voluntary team of teachers share the changes in both philosophy and action that occurred in four years, rather than the principal, modeled the belief in collaboration and empowerment in a high school.

Upon arriving at Osceola High School in 2004, Carol shared with the faculty the need of change so that the school would move from being undistinguished, almost a forgotten school, to being known for its service to students. She met with the teacher leadership team and administrators to hear what they believed needed to change, and together created a vision to be shared consistently with one voice. Carol created a nonnegotiable of change—the faculty determined what the change would be. As they shared, it became clear that low-achieving students, average-achieving students, and high-achieving students could all be served better with higher expectations and research-based instruction.

To accomplish the goals of serving all students better, instructional interventions have been implemented for those performing below grade level in mathematics and reading. Advancement Via Individual Determination (AVID) has been implemented for average students who need more structure and study skills built into their daily instruction. A new expectation for Advanced Placement (AP) teachers is to attend AP professional development if they want to continue teaching AP courses. A philosophical change of inclusion of students into honors (on-grade level/college preparatory) and AP courses versus exclusion and elitism for specially selected students has also taken place. Students are encouraged to enroll in more challenging courses and are not screened out, understanding that more rigor results in greater learning. With more diverse students in advanced classes, the teachers have enhanced their teaching for continued success.

The faculty and administration applied to be a Fundamental School of choice for ninth- and tenth-grade students and was the first in Florida to have this status. A Fundamental School is one whose role is to develop expertise in traditional core content on the part of students. As a result, pre-algebra is no longer taught and has been replaced with the more rigorous course of algebra. There are more students in honors classes, and more in AP courses. As administrators walk through classes, they observe more research-based instruction than in the first three years.

In addition to many teachers attending conferences and outside professional development, within the school, professional development is also provided. Teachers participate in strategy walks within each other's classes to observe their colleagues implementing research-based instruction, so that they can provide feedback and can see expert models within their own hallways. Creating the expectation and norm of learning from each other is a characteristic of schools whose performance regularly increases.

Reorganization of the faculty and staff was also needed to align professional roles with the expectations for enhanced student learning. Like other schools seeking interdisciplinary approaches and more personalization in large schools, Osceola has professional learning communities (PLCs). Each PLC has an administrator, counselor, lead teacher, and classroom teachers. When the PLCs meet, Carol attends and participates. Department chairpersons' roles have changed from administrative to facilitating content learning. Teachers actively study the data on each of their students and design instruction to support success of each.

With the enhanced expectations for student learning and research-based instruction, some faculty chose to leave or were career counseled to make another professional decision. For those who remain, feedback is provided as the administrative team of Carol and four assistant principals walk through classes. According to Maxon (2006, 2009), to improve personnel performance we have to provide courageously authentic feedback; we have to develop an expectation of active caring. At Osceola High School, faculty empowerment has provided the vehicle for continuous improvement through authentic feedback so that the professionals are more expert, resulting in all students achieving at higher levels.

How do they know these second-order changes are worth doing? In 2005–2006 school year, Osceola ranked thirteenth out of sixteen Pinellas School District high schools based on student achievement. By 2007–2008, Osceola had risen to fifth out of sixteen. In tenth-grade reading, 66 percent of Osceola students scored at the proficient level on the Florida Comprehensive Achievement Test (FCAT). In mathematics, 91% scored at the proficient level. In both reading and mathematics, Osceola students outperformed the state average and the district average. Parental participation has increased to the point that more than 800 out of 1,600 parents attend open house and similar meetings! To see the perceptions of the leadership team on how the culture has changed, see Table 2.1.

Table 2.1 Osceola High School Leadership Team: Perceptions of School Culture

Before 2004	2008
Teachers had no control.	Teachers are united.
Teachers were frustrated.	Teachers feel cooperation.
Student discipline was not good.	Student discipline is better.
Chaotic.	Respectful.
Lack of communication.	Collaborative.
Student and teacher attendance not good.	Student and teacher attendance has improved.

Lake Silver Elementary and Special School: Urban

Students: 497   Teachers: 44

Poverty: 68%

ELL: 12%   ESE: 35%

White: 32%   African   Hispanic: 9%
                      American: 55%

LEADER IN ACTION

Cynthia Dodge, Lake Silver Elementary and Special School

> *We had a culture of mediocrity, based on tradition.*

—Cynthia Dodge

Four years earlier, Cynthia Dodge was appointed as principal of a K–5 elementary school also serving the district as a center for students with severe disabilities. When she arrived on campus for the first time, she was struck by the negative climate. The climate felt bad; the building itself was in disrepair and office personnel, paraprofessionals, and teachers projected a sense of resignation. The school sits in a small affluent community within a larger urban district, and it seemed easy for the faculty and staff to blame the school's assigned grade of D from the Florida Department of Education on children bused from a less affluent area. Cynthia's first action was to hang a banner, "Learning is our priority," to send a message of her values and vision that all students would have an excellent learning experience.

The previous principal had been in the role for twenty-two years, and many faculty had similar tenure. Perception was that the primary focus was on the 32 percent of the students who live in the school's immediate neighborhood and whose parents are empowered. Lake Silver had a culture based on a tradition of mediocrity rather than a focus on the 68 percent of the students who receive free- or reduced-lunch benefits. What makes this description curious is that the school sits in a community with parents who love the school, support the school, and will do anything to provide excellent education for their children, but they had no other school experience for comparison.

As a first-year principal, Cynthia made the immediate priority to upgrade the facility to one deserved by the students and faculty. This took two years to complete and the facility is now attractive, inviting, and a healthy place to learn. Renovations included bringing the technology assets to the level expected in 2008 for administrators, teachers, and students alike.

Paraprofessionals, who were the highest paid, did the least meaningful work—made bulletin boards because that is what they liked to do. This practice changed. By the end of year one, Cynthia had reorganized the staff; each now has a specific job description and is held accountable for its fulfillment.

Physical reorganization was necessary with the teachers too. For the second year of her principalship, Cynthia moved thirty-one faculty members' rooms and responsibilities. Along with the physical movement, there was an expectation that all children would receive research-based instruction and high expectations. A ninety-minute, core-reading block was implemented and a new hands-on mathematics series, "Everyday Math," was adopted. These changes were significant curricular and instructional adjustments for the teachers and the paraprofessionals.

In the second year and thereafter, the essential question to base decisions upon is, "What is best for students?" This essential question led to the elimination of ability grouping (which had served to segregate students racially and economically) over the next two years. Teachers are now involved with data study on their students and are held accountable for data-based instructional decisions. Grade-level teams meet weekly to discuss data and related instruction. Faculty meetings (previously nonexistent) always include professional development.

At first, resentment and conflict abounded. Difficult conversations have taken place with faculty and Cynthia provides courageously authentic feedback. During the first three years, 63 percent of the faculty and staff retired, resigned, or were transferred to another school. These changes are positive; they have allowed Cynthia to rebuild the school with adults focused on all students learning at higher levels.

The fourth year brought no turnover in faculty or staff and no team changes. The school's grade for the last two years has been an A. This school is a model for research-based instruction and leadership. Second-order change related to the school culture has been successful.

Cynthia expresses that she could not have been successful as a new principal in such a challenging situation, with such difficult decisions to be made in the best interest of students, without the complete support of her supervisor, the area superintendent. District-level support for tolerating the discomfort of those who do not want to change and prefer the status quo is essential for principals leading change in the most challenging situations.

REFLECTION

The culture of the school or district has a relationship to improvement in student achievement. If the culture is focused on continuous improvement of learning for both adults and students, it tends to have gains in student achievement. When districts or schools do not have such a culture, then it is incumbent on the leader to strategically make structural and organizational changes to influence the culture. All too often, cultures have to change from being focused on the adults, to prioritizing the learning of each student, every day. This change only happens when decision making is made in the best interest of students and not for adult convenience or comfort.

The examples in this chapter represent dramatic changes. Some leaders may not be comfortable with such dramatic change or may lead in districts where they must work more slowly due to union or political constraints. However, the leaders in this text worked successfully within union contracts and with union representatives, and their political environment outside of the union, to accomplish what is best for learning.

The following chapters illustrate other successful changes contributing to the change in culture to one focused on learning. Table 2.2 on page 23 shows each of the leader action themes for second-order change and examples of those actions. It may be helpful in conceptualizing how the themes work together to create a powerful system for change.

PRACTICAL TIPS

- Listen and build trust among faculty, staff, students, and the community.
- Visit classrooms as often as possible and provide authentic feedback.
- Be clear about the high expectations for students and faculty.
- Do not avoid difficult conversations related to curriculum, instruction, and assessment.
- Select one or two priorities related to learning, and then be active and consistent with these priorities.

TRENDS IN FOCUSING CULTURE ON LEARNING AND MAKING DECISIONS FOR LEARNING

1. Focusing on all students learning.

2. High expectations for all students.

3. Strategizing to develop respectful adult and student relationships.

4. Creating clear expectations for research-based instruction and student work.

5. Creating common student assessments by teachers who have the same curriculum responsibilities. This common-assessment practice assists with the identification and consistency of rigor and drives the instructional focus across a grade or content.

6. Studying and discussing grading of student work, including the value of zero.

7. Visiting classrooms and providing feedback often.

8. Providing courageously authentic feedback, and expecting it in return, resulting in a school culture of continual improvement for adults and students alike.

9. Initiating difficult discussions with faculty, staff, and administration about performance to raise the expectations for student learning and to provide clear accountability.

10. Purposefully reorganizing the school, physically and conceptually, to facilitate collaboration and efficiency; combining the best expertise to serve both the needs of students and of the faculty's professional development.

11. Creating small learning communities—probably fewer than eight adults.

HELPFUL TERMS

Ability grouping: Instructional grouping of students based on achievement data. Historically, the groups are stable and do not represent flexible movement to a higher or lower group as students learn.

Active caring: Professional commitment to others in the workplace expecting feedback intended to enhance each other's performance. "I care enough about you professionally to want you to be your best, and I hope you care enough about me professionally to support me in continued growth."

Common assessments: Student assessments developed collaboratively by teachers who teach the same subject or grade, and given with the same grading.

Courageously authentic feedback: Professional feedback that is genuine and provides basis for improved performance. It is not condescending, nor placating, but an accurate representation supported with assistance to improve.

Data days: Professional time set aside for the specific purpose of studying student data with the goal to agree on next steps to close the achievement gap between students achieving and not achieving.

ELL: English Language Learners; English is not the student's primary home language.

ESE: Exceptional Student Education: Special education, not gifted.

Evidence-based instruction (also research-based instruction): instruction, grounded in sound contemporary theory or research which literature suggests would lead to improved learning.

Intervention: Intensive instruction with more time, different instruction, or different resources.

Nonnegotiable: Expectations that are set.

Poverty: Percent of students receiving free- or reduced-lunch benefits.

Professional learning communities (PLCs): Groups of professionals who have the same interest or focus for their professional study.

Research-based instruction: Evidence-based instruction.

Small learning communities (SLCs): Grouping of students into manageable sizes so that each feels significant and receives appropriate attention for success. These may be organized by grade, across content areas (interdisciplinary), or may have a career or interest focus such as the Science and Engineering SLC.

Teachers: Instructional positions, not administrators.

Table 2.2 Focus the Culture on Learning With Leader Action Themes: Examples

Theme	Elementary School	Middle School	High School	Elementary Special School
Focus the Culture on Learning.	Establish clear expectations for teachers.	Ask, is it good for kids and learning?	Teachers voice that the culture has changed.	Banner displays, "Learning is our priority."
Make Decisions for Student Learning.	Strategically organize into small learning communities.	Hold tutoring during lunch, rather than after school.	Promote inclusion vs. elitism and exclusion.	Reorganize faculty/staff. Renovate facility.
Stimulate Intellectual Growth.	Target professional development.	Model professional reading and writing. Expect learning.	Study what is best for nonproficient, proficient, and above-proficient students.	Include ongoing professional development at every faculty meeting.
Personally Invest in the Change.	Develop high level of trust.	Decide 50% lowest grade for homework.	Visit classrooms regularly to provide feedback.	Eliminate nonessential services to address budget deficit.
Expect Collaboration.	Hold data days for collaboratively studying student work/data.	Create behavior leadership team.	Establish nonnegotiable of change—teachers decide. PLCs	Hold weekly grade-level team meetings to plan instruction.

(Continued)

23

Table 2.2 (Continued)

Theme	Elementary School	Middle School	High School	Elementary Special School
Strategize for Consistency.	Meet daily with administrative team. Visit each class twice weekly.	Meet regularly with administrative team who works with teacher team.	Applied to be Fundamental School of Choice. Career counseled those who did not meet expectations.	Institute leadership meetings, classroom visits with feedback.
Expect Data-Based Decision Making.	School uses data objectively to make decisions.	School has minimal teacher turnover, and discipline referrals are down.	Student achievement has grown from being a D school to a B school in four years.	Weekly grade-level teams study ongoing student work/data.
Engage Families.	Parents requested to include middle grades.		Fundamental School requires parental participation.	
Influence Through the Political Environment.		Work actively with the school district.	Seek district support for magnet status and for faculty changes.	Receive essential supervisor support for the changes.

3

Stimulate Intellectual Growth

In Chapter 1, the background research upon which this book is developed was introduced. Chapter 2 presented the central theme—focus the culture of the school on all students learning and do that by making decisions for student learning, not for adult convenience. To accomplish the first two themes, it is essential that the leader is knowledgeable of contemporary research on leadership and learning.

Interestingly, in most of the interviews, the leaders prefaced their comments with research and theory *without any solicitation of the research by the interviewer.* As mentioned in Chapter 2, the interview would begin with the invitation for the leader to share the innovation or change that he believed to be most important at the school or district. As an example, after the leader indicated the need to change the culture of the school, he might add, "We have reorganized into professional learning communities. I have been influenced by the work of DuFour. We are continuing a study group on professional learning communities." This type of response is consistent with the second-order change factor of intellectual stimulation (Marzano, Waters, & McNulty, 2005), "Being knowledgeable about the research and theory regarding the innovation and fostering the knowledge among staff through reading and discussion" (p. 72). Wagner and Kagan (2006) also indicate that leaders who make changes successfully speak from the research.

Clearly, leaders used as examples in this text stay abreast of contemporary thinking through conference attendance, reading, and thoughtful discussions with colleagues. They easily converse about their own professional growth and the professional development for their targeted innovation. Resources that the leaders mentioned as helpful are provided as an additional feature at the end of this chapter, which addresses stimulating intellectual growth, the third leader action theme for second-order change.

One of the first considerations for stimulating intellectual growth is for leaders to participate right alongside those they lead. A retired executive director of high schools in a large district attended to his own professional growth just as he expected principals to attend to opportunities for themselves and for teachers. During a several-year period while I was involved with literacy leadership in his district for principals, literacy coaches, and teachers, I noticed that the director would slide in the back door and begin to participate. After he did this a few times, I started to tease him about checking up on me. He would laugh and say that he had to learn as much as he could because he expected it of the principals. The principals provided him with their schedule of school-based professional development so he always knew what was taking place. This type of leadership participation sent a message to everyone in the high schools that literacy learning in the high schools was important and that everyone should take their literacy learning as seriously as he took his.

Just as the executive director knew he could not lead what he did not know, successful leaders learn along with their colleagues and teachers. In Seminole County Schools, elementary principals are required to attend any professional development attended by their teachers. This district is known for high student achievement and principals learning along with teachers could be part of the district's success strategy.

Leaders' facility with the research supporting the target change seems to make it easier for them to lead others. We generally think about change before we take action. As an example, I know that chocolate and overindulgence results in weight gain, but I am not consistent in acting on this knowledge. Changing behavior is more difficult than cognitive learning.

Worthington School District: Suburban

Students: 9,600   Poverty: 20%

ELL: 4%   ESE: 12%

White: 76%   African   Hispanic: 4%
              American: 8%

Multiracial: 5%   Asian: 7%

Cindy Westover, curriculum leader for reading and language arts in Worthington School District, Ohio, offers an interesting perspective, taking the concept of the knowing-doing gap a level deeper. Cindy shares that during her first year in the district position, she listened to teachers and administrators in each school talk about how reading and language arts were taught. She assumed that what they said accurately described the classrooms, but when she visited classrooms she saw instruction unlike what had been described. In Cindy's words,

"I believe that some teachers know and don't do what they know. But, I also believe that there are many teachers who believe they are using research-based instruction—for example, guided reading—but they are not. They really just have students in groups." The same kind of thing takes place in districts, schools, and classrooms; we often know something and do not choose to act on it for one reason or another. Or, we think we understand a concept and maybe even think we are implementing the concept, but we may not be doing so with fidelity.

With faculty and with other administrators, the leaders are consistent in speaking about the research related to their target change, providing opportunities for learning, and expecting action and accountability for follow-up. The follow-up accountability is where leaders confirm that the expectations are understood and met, or provide feedback and support to create a successful situation. Many use a strategy called "the broken record." They do not allow other important happenings to sway them, and they do not waiver or forget the focus; they are consistent with the message of what is important and why it will work, based on research.

Knowledge of curriculum, evidence-based instruction, and assessment—the first factor of second-order change (Marzano, Waters, & McNulty, 2005)—goes hand in hand with understanding the research and theoretical underpinnings of the target change or innovation. Since most of the target changes have the expectation of influencing gains in student achievement, such knowledge is essential to the success of the implementation and is related to the change in culture noted in Chapter 2. It is also directly related to stimulating intellectual growth. According to Little (1993), professional development should be meaningful, social, and emotionally engaging with ideas, materials, and colleagues. To result in gains in student achievement, the professional development, as in these examples, should be based on data, immediately transferable to the classroom, and with accountability for results. Through various forms of intellectual stimulation, experts have been created within each of the schools and districts to assist with the second-order change implementation, leading to job-embedded professional development.

Examples across the interviews consistently include putting the teachers in positions of respected learners with acknowledgment from others. Doug Reeves's idea of the adult science project reflects this same thinking (2008b). Teachers and administrators engage in action research and report the data, results, and conclusions on three-panel displays. Colleagues participate in a gallery walk or review to learn from each other and to celebrate successes. Annually, the thirteen participating districts of the University of Central Florida-Progress Energy Leadership Institute provide such displays of how the district and schools are using what they have learned in the sessions, and how they measure results. They express enjoyment in receiving feedback from colleagues in other districts while collaboratively learning.

Fort Wayne Community Schools: Urban

Students: 31,600 Poverty: 61%

ELL: 4%   ESE: 9%

White: 56%   African   Hispanic: 11%
                    American: 25%

Multiracial: 3%

LEADER IN ACTION

Linda Roman, Fort Wayne Community Schools

All targets get measured; everything is data driven, even district professional development.

—Linda Roman

Fort Wayne Community Schools, Indiana, was not achieving in literacy at an acceptable level in the middle and high schools. Linda Roman, director of professional development, determined that literacy leadership and learning for administrators and teams of teachers might be helpful professional development, leading to a better understanding of research as a basis for taking action. Linda provided these workshops for volunteer teams a number of times. By providing professional development for teams, the administrators and teachers together hear the same message and have time to strategize within the professional-development day for how to move the school forward in literacy learning. Upon leaving the professional development, the principal and teacher team share with other faculty the concepts and ideas they learn and would like to consider implementing in the school. Over time, participating principals began to take ownership and professional development became school based, including in-class collegial literacy coaching.

This professional development is an example of meaningful engagement with professional colleagues, building capacity for change. It begins with district leadership sensitive to how to create ownership at the school level through adult learning. It is initiated at the district level based on data and successfully transferred to the school level with district support.

Round Lake Charter Elementary School: Rural

Students: 1,166 Teachers: 75

Poverty: 45%

ELL: 14%   ESE: 12%

White: 64%   African   Hispanic: 21%
                    American: 11%

LEADER IN ACTION

Dale Moxley, Round Lake Charter Elementary School

When I let the teachers volunteer to participate and select the book to study, their enthusiasm was surprising. Book studies have become the norm and sustain the changes.

—Dale Moxley

The school where Dale Moxley is principal is one that serves an attendance zone, but is a charter school under the auspices of the school district. It is acknowledged as a high-performing school and thus continually grows by parent requests or parents moving into the attendance zone. Dale acknowledges that the students' high performance left the faculty with no sense of urgency to learn more and to improve their instruction. However, even in high-performing schools, there are students who can be stretched a little more and those who need more intervention.

In Dale's efforts to bring high-quality professional development to the faculty, a nationally recognized consultant met with the faculty to discuss vocabulary instruction. After the experience, teachers were positive about making changes in vocabulary instruction, but over time, they seemed to go back to the way they instructed vocabulary before the consultation.

Determined to push vocabulary improvement forward, two books were purchased for book studies: *Building Academic Vocabulary* (Marzano & Pickering, 2005) and *Building Background Knowledge* (Marzano, 2004). Grade-level teams were expected to meet regularly to have these book studies, while faculty generated discussion questions to guide the meetings. Teachers enjoyed the book studies, but more importantly, they implemented the research-based vocabulary strategies that now represent the normal expectation in the school. The book study is a vehicle for teachers to have intellectual stimulation with research and engage in substantive discussions with valued colleagues. It is a respectful and safe learning environment for the adults.

With this positive experience, teachers have asked for more book studies. They have progressed to choosing their own professional books and forming their own groups. They implement ideas from the book studies and invite feedback as colleagues (Taylor & Moxley, 2008). Dale has observed that this process enhances the students' learning, and the student achievement continues in a positive trend.

LEADER IN ACTION

Harold Border, Hunter's Creek Middle School

> *Expect professional development for yourself, your faculty, and your staff.*

—Harold Border

Hunter's Creek Middle School: Suburban		
Students: 1,038	Teachers: 58	
Poverty: 41%	ELL: 19%	ESE: 9%
White: 39%	African American: 6%	Hispanic: 40%
Other: 15%		

As principal, Harold Border has high expectations while focusing on relationships, rewards, and recognition. How has professional development under his leadership changed? As a first-year principal, faculty participated in common professional development during their planning periods. This went well and the teachers exhibited expertise in instruction and application of the target concepts, such as literacy infusion. In the second year, individuals selected which professional development to attend. The third-year teachers formed into professional learning communities and determined their own focus of study, such as grading. By the fourth year, professional learning communities created online learning, continued face-to-face discussions once each month, and individuals voluntarily attended professional development of their choice.

Action research has also become a component of professional development at Hunter's Creek. In 2007–2008, fifteen teachers participated in action research, and every teacher had the opportunity. The following year, individual professional development plans (required by the school district) included action research and were required to be data based. Examples include teachers creating common and end-of-chapter assessments in content areas—assisting with the understanding of what represents rigor. Another example is the sixth-grade teachers' focus on asking higher levels of questions that reflect synthesis, analysis, application, and evaluation. Science and mathematics teachers triangulate the data on grade-level benchmarks, the Florida Comprehensive Assessment Test, and common assessments. These types of study deepen the teachers' thinking about their daily work. By working together, a friendly accountability—colleague to colleague—unofficially takes place.

To support the teacher-driven professional development and action research, Harold follows up with rewards and recognitions for excellent implementations. He writes personal notes to teachers as many administrators do. Going beyond the typical, he sends letters home to the teachers' families telling them what excellent work the teachers are doing.

How does Harold know that his strategy of high expectations, focusing on relationships and respectful professional development, has worked? Understandably, he has received an overwhelmingly positive response from individuals whose families received the positive comments. In the 2008–2009 school year, there were eight professional learning communities. Only five teachers continued to give zeros for homework, and changes in classroom instruction and assessment have been observed.

Orange County Public Schools: Urban		
Students: 174,000		
Poverty: 58%		
ELL: 19%	ESE: 15%	
White: 34%	African American: 27%	Hispanic: 31%
Asian: 4%	Multiracial: 3%	

LEADER IN ACTION

Janie Phelps, Orange County Public Schools

> *I learned more about history and literacy in these three days than in my entire career.*
>
> —Middle School Social Studies Teacher

Janie Phelps, the coordinator for social studies in Orange County Public Schools was faced with multiple challenges beyond standards-based curriculum alignment. She was charged with improving social studies learning while integrating literacy into the teachers' daily work. By collaborating with social studies scholars and educators at the University of Central Florida and the Central Florida Regional History Center, she applied for and has received a grant to address the identified needs. The grant began in 2008 and will continue for a five-year period. The design of the grant has multiple layers of objectives for professional development: deepen knowledge of U.S. history and social studies, enhance knowledge and practice of research-based social studies pedagogy, and enhance knowledge of practice of research-based literacy infusion. These objectives may sound almost impossible to achieve and, at first, may have been without a systematic and thoughtful implementation.

Teachers volunteer to participate as do teacher mentors who are National Board Certificated Teachers. It is anticipated that about fifty teachers each year for up to five years will participate, creating a critical mass for enhancing social studies learning and literacy learning. Most learning experiences take place outside of the school day with teacher compensation, but some provide release time from school. All of the incentives are grant funded.

Implementation includes high-quality professional development at the Orange Regional History Center related to the project objectives. Ongoing book studies on both historical content and pedagogy cement the community of learners between the monthly face-to-face colloquiums. The formal professional development days are followed by in-school coaching visits by the literacy consultant, accompanied by Janie and mentor teachers. This model is designed to build capacity for ongoing collegial coaching with the mentor teachers and eventually will be expanded to other teachers within each school. In the summer following each year of professional development and collegial coaching, teachers participate in an eleven-day fieldtrip to Washington, D.C. and historical sites.

It is too early to measure the results in student data, but the feedback from teachers and their principals is that this experience is a success. In visiting the schools and the teachers' classrooms, I have observed very skillful instruction by novice social studies teachers. Partnering to promote high-quality professional development, intellectual stimulation by history scholars, and personal coaching on improved pedagogy and literacy infusion is changing how the teachers teach, hence improving student engagement and enjoyment of social studies.

REFLECTION

With the long hours and overwhelming responsibilities, school leaders who are successfully making second-order change stay abreast of current research and trends in learning. They seek out experiences for their own professional growth, read professional literature, and engage in collaborative discussions with colleagues. Just as they attend to their professional growth, they strategize for ongoing professional development, in all of its forms, with their colleagues. Table 3.1 shows how the capacity for professional development may take place. If the adults are not growing professionally, then how could it be expected that student achievement would increase?

Table 3.1   Progression of Professional Development: Example

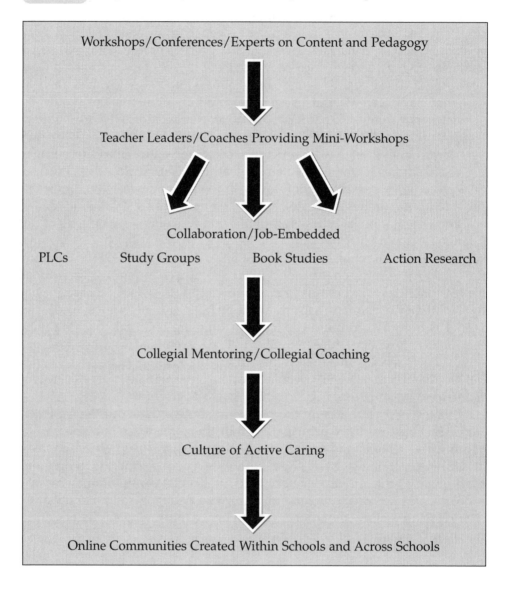

PRACTICAL TIPS

- Become an expert in the target change. Read books, attend conference sessions, communicate with experts, and visit schools and districts where the target change has been successful.
- Evaluate the teachers' and administrators' knowing-doing gap for the target change. Target professional development for this gap.

- Use student-achievement data to drive professional development—study groups, professional learning communities, workshops, and action research.
- Reward and recognize faculty and administrators for implementing new learning.

TRENDS IN STIMULATING INTELLECTUAL GROWTH

1. Designing data-based, district professional development to build capacity in schools.

2. Data-based, school-level professional development.

3. Creating experts within the schools—teacher leaders.

4. Collegial coaching.

5. Action research.

6. Book studies and study groups.

7. Professional learning communities.

8. Both leaders and teachers facilitating and participating in professional development.

9. Being accountable for acting on what is learned in professional development.

10. Rewarding and recognizing implementation of new learning.

11. Partnering with other nonprofit educational organizations.

HELPFUL TERMS

Action research: School-based research where the topic to be studied is identified, the implementation of a strategy takes place, and the result is measured. For example, in science, a teacher focused on asking higher-order questions for written responses. The result was higher achievement in science (writing is thinking) and higher achievement in writing.

Book study: Two or more select the same book to read, reflect, and discuss. Typically, there is a schedule of when chapters are to be read and who will lead the discussion. Teachers usually try out the strategies in the book and share the results at the book study sessions.

Gallery walk: Strategy where work is displayed as in an art gallery and participants or students walk around the gallery gathering ideas, making notes, and/or discussing what they see. One technique is for participants/students to put sticky-note comments on the work to quickly provide authentic feedback.

Job-embedded: Professional development that relates directly to the work and is built into the normal work—classroom coaching, feedback, strategy walks, book studies, action research, etc.

Literacy coach: A teacher whose job is to provide teacher leadership and professional coaching to other teachers on literacy related instruction—phonics, phonemic awareness, comprehension vocabulary, fluency, speaking, and writing.

RESOURCES FOR LEADERS

Dana, N. F., & Yendol-Silva, D. (2003). *The reflective educator's guide to classroom research.* Thousand Oaks, CA: Corwin.

Dufour, R., & Eaker, R. (1998). *Professional learning communities at work.* Bloomington, IN: National Educational Service.

Fullan, M. (2006). *Turnaround leadership.* San Francisco: Wiley.

Glickman, C. D. (2002). *Leadership for learning: How to help teachers succeed.* Alexandria, VA: Association for Supervision and Curriculum Development.

Marzano, R. J. (2004). *Building background knowledge.* Alexandria, VA: Association for Supervision and Curriculum Development.

Marzano, R. J., & Pickering, D. J. (2005). *Building academic vocabulary.* Alexandria, VA: Association for Supervision and Curriculum Development.

Marzano, R. J., Waters, T., & McNulty, B. A. (2005). *School leadership that works.* Alexandria, VA: Association for Supervision and Curriculum Development.

Moxley, D. E., & Taylor, R. T. (2006). *Literacy coaching: A handbook for school leaders.* Thousand Oaks, CA: Corwin and National Association of Secondary School Principals.

Peterson, K. D., & Deal, T. E. (2002). *The shaping school culture fieldbook.* San Francisco: Jossey-Bass.

Reeves, D. B. (2004). *Accountability for learning: How teachers and school leaders can take charge.* Alexandria, VA: Association for Supervision and Curriculum Development.

Reeves, D. B. (2006). *The learning leader: How to focus school improvement for better results.* Alexandria, VA: Association for Supervision and Curriculum Development.

Reeves, D. B. (Ed.). (2008a). *Ahead of the curve: The power of assessment to transform teaching and learning.* Bloomington, IN: Solution Tree.

Reeves, D. B. (2008b). *Reframing teacher leadership to improve your school.* Alexandria, VA: Association for Supervision and Curriculum Development.

Schmoker, M. (2006). *Results now: How we can achieve unprecedented achievements in teaching and learning.* Alexandria, VA: Association for Supervision and Curriculum Development.

Taylor, R. T. (2007). *Improving reading, writing, and content learning for students in grades 4–12.* Thousand Oaks, CA: Corwin.

Taylor, R. T., & Collins, V. D. (2003). *Literacy leadership for Grades 5–12.* Alexandria, VA: Association for Supervision and Curriculum Development.

Taylor, R. T., & Gunter, G. A. (2006). *The K–12 literacy leadership fieldbook.* Thousand Oaks, CA: Corwin.

Tomlinson, C. A., & Allan, S. D. (2000). *Leadership for differentiating schools and classrooms.* Alexandria, VA: Association for Supervision and Curriculum Development.

Wagner, T., & Kagan, R. (2006). *Change leadership.* San Francisco: Wiley.

4

Invest Personally in the Change

The fourth leader action theme for second-order change clearly illustrates how gains in student achievement are the priority, with the leader personally directing this change. Investing personally in the change might be automatically presumed, but in past decades, executive leadership at the district and school levels have often delegated the work to others. Leaders may have remained a little distant from the processes and procedures necessary to make the changes and perhaps focused more on global and political issues. In contrast, there appears to be a relationship between the personal investment of the leader, even at the executive levels, in the change and the results in student achievement from the implementation. These leaders chose to delegate other important responsibilities to their assistants, curriculum leaders, instructional coaches, and teacher leaders. But, the leaders personally led the target change. Personal investment is evidenced by deep knowledge of the target change, continually speaking about the target change, as well as participation in the development, implementation, related professional development, and monitoring of the change and its results. As such, this chapter addresses investing personally in second-order change, the fourth leadership theme.

Pine Crest Elementary School: Urban

Students: 834   Teachers: 69

Poverty: 85%   ELL: 12%   ESE: 16%

White: 37%   African   Hispanic: 23%
              American: 34%

Multiracial: 5% Asian: 1%

When Carol Chanter became principal of Pine Crest Elementary School, she faced one of the lowest student-achievement results in the large district. Her philosophy was a contrast to the previous principal's. He had retained nonperforming students in their current grade level, while she believed in remediation and moving the students forward academically to the next grade level.

Since this was an important philosophical change for faculty, Carol personally had discussions with teachers and created the intervention plan. Students in danger of being retained received intensive intervention—such as being grouped into a small, intensive class with a paraprofessional in addition to the classroom teacher. Each student had an individual plan and Carol met with the students' teachers regularly to review the progress or discuss another intervention, if needed. When teachers had small-group guided reading, students did not go into learning/literacy centers to work independently. Instead, other certified teachers came into the class so that all students were in a small, guided reading group at the same time with a certified teacher, not a paraprofessional as is often the case in primary classrooms. Carol also met with teacher teams monthly to receive and to provide feedback.

These planning and monitoring sessions could easily have been delegated to other leaders at the school—assistant principal, instructional coach, Title 1 coordinator—but Carol knew that she had to personally take on the charge for significant improvements to occur. While Carol was at Pine Crest Elementary, the students' reading and writing performance improved, representing incremental, ongoing growth.

Another personal investment is of the leader's time and energy. Common perceptions that leaders who work in high schools may be less likely to be instructional leaders were not confirmed with the principals I visited. One of the consistencies throughout the interviews and visits is that the successful principals visit classrooms regularly, regardless of whether the school is elementary, middle, or high school. The larger the school, the more strategically these visits take place and a little less often, but they are a priority nonetheless. Frequently, these classroom visits are documented as classroom walkthroughs or strategy walks on an instrument that allows trends to be analyzed across the school and across different observers. They are neither social nor symbolic visits; they are purposeful and deliberate, targeting specific curricular, instructional, and assessment changes.

An outstanding example of a suburban principal who personally invests in the changes is John Wright. He has created a student-focused high school culture and asks, "What is best for students?" The fall of 2008 was the beginning of the eighth year of Timber Creek High School and his principalship there. Since the school is perceived to be excellent, it has grown to over 4,400 students and will soon have a relief high school to reduce the student population—but students want to stay at

Timber Creek High School: Suburban		
Students: 4,426	Teachers: 245	
Poverty: 34%	ELL: 10%	ESE: 12%
White: 48%	African American: 10%	Hispanic: 31%
Asian: 4%	Multiracial: 2%	

Timber Creek. In fact, there are 1,400 students who take advanced academic classes each morning during zero period (7:00 a.m.), before the beginning of the official school day.

At Timber Creek, John leads possibility thinking. As ideas are brought to John, he asks, "What do we need to do to accomplish the idea if it is best for students?" rather than "This has never been done or I don't know if we can get permission. . . ." One example of his possibility thinking is that there are students who want to take Chinese as a foreign language, so the school offered it against district advisement. By 2008, there were two full-class sections of Chinese and the students scored 5s on the Advanced Placement Exam, indicating success in the course. Arabic language is the newest curricular addition, and when approaching its inclusion, John was informed that it could not be taught because the state had no Arabic teacher certification/licensure. Since he still thought Arabic as a course offering would be in the best interest of students, John worked with the Florida Department of Education to create a teacher certification waiver so that a qualified person could teach the course. Possibility thinking, which assumes positive intent of other decision makers, opens the door for positive changes for students.

Not only does John focus on the high-performing students, but he also ensures that all students at risk of failing have a mentor through a program called Wolf Watch. The wolf is the school's mascot, and Wolf Watch is a student monitoring and mentoring program where John, all administrators, faculty, and staff—including the custodians and security personnel—monitor and mentor students. They work individually with students monitoring their work and grades, providing assistance and support when needed.

Rather than being satisfied with regular class visits and walkthrough observations, John insists that he and the administrative team regularly teach classes. His purpose is to maintain their credibility as teachers and stay in touch with students, curriculum, and instruction. For example, during the spring semester of 2008, a teacher had to leave suddenly. Rather than hiring a long-term substitute teacher, John and the administrators divided the teacher's classes and each taught a class for several weeks. Not only was this impressive to the faculty, parents, and students, but it also guided decision making in the best interest of students. As the leadership team discussed their experiences, it became apparent that the course needed curricular and instructional modifications. To serve students better, changes to raise the rigor of the course and the instructional strategies were subsequently made for the opening of the next school year. This example represents personal investment in the change, not commonplace delegation to others, particularly prevalent in large high schools. Timber Creek Wolves are making academic progress with John's personal investment.

Adairville K–8 School: Rural/small town

Students: 341   Teachers: 30

Poverty: 50%

ELL: 1%   ESE: 16%

White: 89%   African   Hispanic: 1%
American: 7%

LEADER IN ACTION

Paul Sansom, Adairville K–8 School

We needed to play well together.

—Paul Sansom

In rural areas, like Adairville K–8 School in central Kentucky, there are excellent schools serving students well. Paul Sansom had just finished the third year as principal when we talked. In the five previous years, I had been in the school a number of times and therefore was familiar with the community, school, and strides made by the teachers and students. In addition to the demographic information offered here, only about 5 percent of the community holds college degrees, indicating a relatively low education level of the families.

Before becoming principal, Paul served as the assistant principal at Adairville; he therefore had intimate knowledge of the strengths and weaknesses within the school. Paul was candid in sharing that he focuses his efforts on improving faculty relations through improving student achievement, hence, "We need to play well together." Trends identified in Chapters 2 and 3 include focusing on respectful relationships, professional learning communities, common assessments, common instructional plans, collegial professional development, and data study. All of these trends require that the adults communicate respectfully and get along well as professional colleagues. I have observed the changes as Paul has attended to these relationships while at the same time improving student achievement.

Paul models respectfulness for the faculty and students. He uses every chance to provide positive feedback. He openly states to the faculty and staff that they will treat each other in positive ways. In his "Week at a Glance" memo, he emphasizes pride in their excellence and professional work, including helping one another. Although nonrenewal can be politically sensitive in a rural stable community, and finding quality replacements is difficult, teachers who did not adopt Paul's philosophy of respect and working well together have not been renewed. Paul believes that the culture of the school has become more positive, and that there is a good feeling in the school, to which I attest.

Creating the culture of working well together, first of all, makes coming to work more pleasurable, but it also lays the foundation to enhance student learning. Teachers share common planning time and plan their instruction together as well as their classroom assessments. Primary teachers (Grades K–3) plan their reading centers together, making sure that they are rigorous, address one of the reading components (phonics, phonemic awareness, vocabulary, fluency, comprehension) or writing, and have an assessment that young children can complete independently. In visiting classroom to classroom, I easily saw the coherence in the teachers' instruction within each grade and commonality in pedagogy grade to grade—evidence of the collaborative relationships that have developed.

Second-order changes have been implemented to target essential content and learning—reading, mathematics, and technology. In contrast to each teacher generating her own curriculum and instruction, a core-reading series has been adopted and implemented in kindergarten through sixth grade supporting consistency. Reading interventions have been put into place in primary grades in the student's classroom and in Grades 4–8 as an intensive reading intervention class.

To improve mathematics, the school participates in a mathematics alliance with the regional service agency. Teachers learn more about the content of mathematics as well as the pedagogy for improving learning in mathematics. This is particularly important since there is abundant research on the lack of elementary teachers' deep mathematical understanding. This is either due to lack of interest or lack of mathematical coursework, so enhancing mathematical knowledge is essential and complementary to enhancing pedagogical skill. Research supports that when knowledge and pedagogy improve, so does student achievement.

Expectations that teachers will use technology for assessment and instruction were new in 2007. By 2009, it is the norm and students have learning blogs and produce photo journals of their work. Technology has invigorated the learning for both the students and teachers.

In a short time, reading achievement has dramatically increased, according to Dynamic Indicators of Basic Early Literacy Skills (DIBELS), Group Reading and Diagnostic Exam (GRADE), and the Scholastic Reading Inventory (SRI). What is more apparent in visiting classrooms is that instruction has changed to reflect more research-based practice. The common planning is evidenced by visiting classrooms of the same grade level. Not only does an observer see aligned, direct teacher instruction, but also aligned intervention groups and learning/reading centers. Students in reading intervention are engaged and are making progress. Today, students at Adairville K–8 School achieve better than some schools with higher levels of parent education and economic support.

Phillip O. Berry Academy of Technology: Urban		
Students: 1,084	Teachers: 95	
Poverty: 52%	ELL: 4%	ESE: 7%
White: 9%	African American: 77%	Hispanic: 8%
Asian: 3%	Multiracial: 3%	

LEADER IN ACTION

Donald Fennoy, Phillip O. Berry Academy of Technology

> *I had to change the expectations and beliefs held by students, parents, and teachers.*

—Donald Fennoy

Like many of his successful counterparts, this assignment is Donald Fennoy's first principal experience. Phillip O. Berry Academy of Technology in Charlotte, North Carolina, is a magnet school built at the cost of over $80,000,000. However, in 2007, the school attracted only 400 students. With this enormous financial investment, district leaders wanted to increase both student enrollment and student achievement. Although students were required to read at grade level to be accepted to the school, their reading levels declined after enrollment. Donald was the choice to take on this charge since he had a history as an assistant principal of helping all students to be more successful, particularly students of color and poverty. He also knows how to change teachers' beliefs about students to believe that the students can be more successful. This change in the teachers' beliefs leads teachers to provide more rigorous expectations and instruction.

According to Donald, he has changed the attitudes of the students, parents, and faculty. Their former expectations for themselves were low. Everyone needed higher expectations for students, including the students. Curriculum, instruction, assessment, and student work did not represent rigorous expectations.

He addresses these concerns directly with faculty, parents, and students. With students, he talks to them in small groups, large groups, and individually about how little they expect of themselves and that they should set their goals higher. He motivates them through personal engagement to enroll in more challenging classes and to work harder while in the classes. Donald speaks to students from a position of personal experience, as he has a similar background being an African-American male raised by a single mother without financial assets.

Faculty is another challenge. With teachers, Donald has had difficult conversations and some have chosen to leave; others have chosen to demonstrate higher expectations and provide students with more rigorous work. Now, counselors sit down with students to complete college admission and scholarship applications since their families might not have the knowledge and skills to present information in its best light. Previously, these applications were only posted on a bulletin board. It was up to the students to secure and complete the applications.

Donald also models what he expects. He does not send teachers to Advanced Placement (AP) workshops. Instead, he attends the workshops with them. By being part of the AP team, he reinforces expectations for inclusion of more diverse students in the AP classes, enhances research-based instruction, and supports rigorous assessment. Faculty attitudes have begun to change toward the students and toward their professional responsibility to assist the students in being successful in challenging courses.

How does Donald know that his personal involvement has yielded results? Two years after arriving as principal, the student enrollment has increased from 400 students to a projection of over 1,300 for the 2009–2010 school year. The 200 graduates in 2008 received more than $5.5 million in scholarships. Advanced Placement and district assessment scores are improving as are numbers of scholarships awarded.

LEADER IN ACTION

Bill Vogel, Seminole County Public Schools

> *Reading is the centerpiece of our high schools.*
>
> —Bill Vogel

Seminole County Public Schools: Suburban

Students: 65,299	Poverty: 34%
ELL: 16%	ESE: 15%
White: 58%	African American: 13% — Hispanic: 18%
Asian: 4%	Other: 7%

In 2004, Superintendent Bill Vogel determined that his diverse district's perception of high achievement might be jeopardized by reading achievement at the high school level. He believed that the level of achievement did not reflect the potential of the students. It certainly was not acceptable to him, the community, or the principals. Bill committed to improving high school reading achievement; he led the charge and was involved in each step of the process. He invited me to attend a meeting of high school principals and district administrators on high school reading achievement where I heard him announce, "Reading is the centerpiece of our high schools." This message was followed by strategic development, implementation, and evaluation of a plan reflecting the commitment.

The principals, who are exceptional in every way, listened, but raised the issue of their own lack of knowledge on research related to literacy learning, as well the lack of literacy expertise of the faculty, other administrators, and staff. Reading implementation at the high school level is second-order change—change in philosophy, expectations, resources, curriculum, instruction, student work, and assessment. As Bill engaged in conversation about literacy learning with the school and district leaders, he turned to me to provide a brief overview of adolescent literacy learning and literacy leadership. From then on, the group engaged in learning about literacy leadership and literacy learning at the high school level.

To support the successful implementation of the high school literacy plan, Bill provides funding for a literacy coach in each of the high schools and for professional development. These coaches collaboratively develop professional development for the teachers. This literacy professional development is contextualized to each academic area and presented to content teachers (mathematics, science, social studies) in content groups across schools, which turns out to be very effective. Literacy coaches are in each school so they follow up with job-embedded professional development and coaching.

The next step, which is significant, is that Bill invited the Florida Center for Reading Research (FCRR) to partner with the school district on research project for high school reading intervention. The project was jointly designed by the school district and FCRR, and had three research-based reading interventions and a control reading intervention of whatever the school chose. For a three-year period, the reading intervention research project continued. Results provided contextualized data on which interventions were more effective with which students within that school district. The results guided the district to target specific student levels of achievement with specific reading interventions. For example, nonfluent readers have one reading intervention, but fluent readers who read below proficient have a different intervention. This level of specificity for targeting particular students with specific research-based interventions is fairly unusual across high schools outside of this school district.

These changes can be seen when visiting the district's high schools. Each principal and administrator easily converse about literacy learning, reading interventions, monitoring assessments, and writing. They can describe instructional practices that work best for students reading at different levels of proficiency. Furthermore, the literacy coaches have grown from providing initial professional development workshops to classroom coaching and to providing literacy coaching based on current student-monitoring data specific to each school.

The end result of more high school students reading at a higher level is a continual process, but the district has made great gain. In 2005–2006, the percent of ninth-grade students making reading gains on the Florida Comprehensive Assessment Test (FCAT) reading ranged from 62–72 percent across the eight high schools. Of the bottom quartile of students, the percent making gains on FCAT reading ranged from 50–68 percent. District means for percent of students reading at the proficient level rose from 47 percent in 2005 to 60 percent in 2008 at the ninth-grade level, and from 69 percent in 2005 to 77 percent in 2008 at the tenth-grade level. Those who are familiar with the challenge to improve high school reading know that this data indicates that the implementation is successful.

There are many district and school administrators, teachers, and teacher leaders involved with this second-order change. It is strategic on every level and a continuous improvement process. However, it is very unusual for a superintendent of a large district to get involved this intimately with a change. Yet Bill was present and involved in every step of the way. The success of reading implementation in the district's high schools is attributed to Bill's personal investment in the entire change—from the beginning and ongoing. For those wanting to explore more, the article, "Systematically Making Reading the Center of High School" (Taylor& Chanter, 2008) offers additional insight on Bill's efforts.

REFLECTION

There are those who believe that leaders spend time with what they know most about, or with whatever they have the most comfort. The rest of the responsibilities are delegated to other capable leaders. This description fits the schools and districts *not* making significant change and gains in student achievement. In schools and districts making significant change and gains in student achievement, the leaders step beyond their comfort levels and develop knowledge and expertise in areas essential to improving student learning. The outer band of Table 1.3 (page 6) illustrates the components of the second-order changes in which leaders personally invest their time and energy sending the message of importance. They delegate other responsibilities that do not need the advocacy and modeling of such a high level of leadership.

PRACTICAL TIPS

- Lead the priority change and delegate less important tasks.
- Actively engage with the faculty, staff, students, and community related to the target change.

TRENDS IN MAKING A PERSONAL INVESTMENT

1. Personally leading the target change.
2. Becoming an expert in the target change.
3. Delegating less important responsibilities.
4. Modeling what is expected of others.
5. Attending all meetings and sessions with teachers.
6. Regularly visiting classrooms regardless of the grade levels served.
7. Progress monitoring learning throughout the school year.
8. Thinking of possibilities and assuming positive intent of others.
9. Asking, "What do we need to implement what is best for students?"
10. Seeking partnerships to support research-based decision making.
11. Making the school attractive to parents, students, and teachers.

Table 4.1   Invest Personally in the Change: Examples and Nonexamples

Nonexamples	Examples
Leader delegates improvement of student achievement to teacher leaders and administrators and does not follow up.	Leader regularly meets with the literacy coach, teacher leaders, and administrators to monitor improvements.
Because the leader's academic background is different from the content area tested, the responsibility for improvement is delegated.	Leader seeks opportunities to learn latest research about targeted areas of learning: reading, mathematics, science, social studies, and writing. Leader facilitates and participates in discussions and decision making related to improvements in student achievement.
Leader accepts ineffective work by faculty, staff, and administrators to avoid conflict and discontent.	Leader has difficult conversations with employees related to student learning.
Leader visits classes when time allows.	Leader strategizes to be in each classroom regularly and to provide authentic feedback.
Leader attends leadership professional development, but not faculty professional development.	Leader attends and even leads faculty professional development. Leader follows up professional development with class visits to note implementation.
Leader accepts budget or curriculum decisions made by others.	Leader engages in active discourse and possibility thinking to make curriculum relevant and to seek budget enhancements through outside sources, if needed.
Leader approves innovations by faculty, staff, and administrators, but does not actively participate.	Leader initiates and follows through with innovations to serve students better.
Because of time constraints and administrative responsibilities, leader does not teach students.	Leader embraces opportunities to teach students, even for brief amounts of time, to remain in touch with the implementation of curriculum, instruction, assessment and challenges faced by faculty and staff.
As the new person to the school, leader accepts the culture and practices of the school that have long been in place.	As a new person to the school, leader makes it clear that the culture of the school will be a healthy one for teachers, parents, and students and is not hesitant to make decisions and take action to that end.

HELPFUL TERMS

Classroom walkthrough: Purposefully and deliberately visiting classrooms for a few minutes to monitor target curriculum, instruction, assessment, student work, and to provide feedback.

Control group: In research, a group who does not experience the target treatment.

Core-reading time: Daily block of time, usually at least ninety minutes, reserved for reading instruction.

Learning centers: Stations within a classroom for individual or small groups of students to review or practice concepts, skills, or content introduced by the teacher.

Nonexample: Different from the target concept.

Primary grades: Prekindergarten through third grades.

Proficient: Target level of achievement determined by each state and used for accountability under No Child Left Behind Act of 2001. May be above, at, or below grade level and varies by state.

Progress monitoring: Ongoing assessment of student learning throughout the school year, generally in mathematics, reading, and/or writing.

Reading center: Learning center for practice focusing on phonics, phonemic awareness, comprehension, vocabulary, fluency, or writing.

Reading components: Phonics, phonemic awareness, vocabulary, fluency, and comprehension.

Reading interventions: Curriculum, instruction, resources, student work, and assessment for students reading below an identified level.

Rigor: Level of difficulty, level of thinking, and level of challenge.

Zero period: Optional class period before the official beginning of the school day.

5

Collaborate to Optimize Success

In each of the previous chapters, examples of collaboration were provided based on focusing the culture on learning, making decisions for student learning, and implementing professional development. Professional collaboration is central to the success of the leaders represented in this book, whether the leaders are at the district or school level. Professional collaboration means purposeful thinking and discussion to seek solutions while assisting one another to be successful in the process. In this book, formalized professional learning communities (DuFour & Eaker, 1998; Eaker, DuFour, & DuFour, 2002) represent collaborations in the form of grade-level teams, content curriculum teams, cross-disciplinary teams, temporary groups, or task forces. These collaborative groups or teams are often colleagues who have determined that collaboration is the best way to be most effective. Leaders use collaboration as a way to provide creativity and ownership in the implementation of nonnegotiable expectations, not necessarily to set the expectations. In fact, collaboration was frequently cited as a nonnegotiable expectation. Remember Paula St. Francis and Carol Moore in Chapter 2? Because of the frequency leaders identify the expectation of collaboration, its use is embedded in the scenarios shared in the other chapters as well, but discussed in depth here.

Leaders are purposeful and deliberate in creating expectations for collaboration. They incorporate characteristics identified by Katzenbach and Smith (1993) of high-performing teams: shape purpose in response to demand or opportunity, translate common purpose into measurable goals, maintain a manageable size, develop mix of expertise, commit to the working relationship, and hold themselves collectively accountable. Collective accountability is absent from less effective collaboration. Additionally, these leaders do not expect teachers and administrators to have discussion without clear guidelines; the expectations for collaboration are specific. Resource C provides an example of expectations.

Mike Blasewitz, principal of Winter Springs High School, shared an example of the nonnegotiable for collaboration with increased annual accountability. The first year, 2005–2006, he describes as "soft" implementation. The expectation of collaboration was shared with supporting research on how collaboration benefits students and teachers. This sharing assisted in dealing with the resistance; high school teachers are used to being independent in their work. Discussions related to collaboration took place during all leadership team, department, and faculty meetings to continually clarify the expectations and to be sure all of those in leadership spoke with one voice.

Winter Springs High School: Suburban		
Students: 2,198	Teachers: 148	
Poverty: 31%	ELL: 2%	ESE: 12%
White: 65%	African American: 10%	Hispanic: 19%
Multiracial: 4%	Asian: 2%	

As teachers began to have collaborative sessions, they realized they needed research to support the discussions. Rather than the teachers searching for research, the administrators searched and provided relevant and related articles for each collaborative team. Administrators wanted the teams to feel supported and empowered to learn and make decisions to improve learning.

Accountability for collaboration has been phased in and increased annually. Eaker, DuFour, and Dufour (2002) and DuFour and Eaker (1998) clarify the leader's role in professional learning communities to monitor and to develop a system of accountability. At Winter Springs High School, each collaborative team submitted an end-of-the-year summary of their study experience after the first year. During the second year, teams were expected to meet monthly and submit minutes of each meeting, a year-end summary, and the results. At the end of that year, forty-four teachers were assigned to different classrooms to cluster collaborative teams near each other to support casual, ongoing discussions for the following year. Accountability was enhanced for the third year. The expectation of common instructional plans and assessment was the purpose of the collaborations, and is supported in the work of Reeves (2006) as important to enhancing learning. This worked well and about fifty teachers visited each other's classes and learned from the modeling observed, collegially coaching each other. At the end of the third year, seventeen teachers requested that their classrooms be moved to facilitate collaboration, indicating that the collaborative process has become a valued norm at the school.

Mike believes that this purposeful collaboration with accountability for results impacts student achievement. In the tenth grade, 93 percent of students scored at the proficient level in 2008. Reading, mathematics, and writing all have improved. Mike, like any excellent leader, reflects that there is still work to be done, teams to enhance, and collaboration to improve.

Betsy Butler became principal of Mila Elementary School in July 2007. Although the school is a Title 1 school, students are making gains in achievement. Because the mobility rate is great and the students frequently move among a set of neighboring elementary schools, Betsy and the four other community school principals created the "super professional learning community" (super PLC). This PLC meets formally each month in grade-level teacher teams. Teachers and administrators share with each other, then have follow-up communications and professional coaching via e-mail and telephone. The super PLC assists students who move among these schools to have consistency, but also expands the range of learning of all of the adults. The super PLC was awarded the Professional Development of the Year Award by the Florida Staff Development Council in 2008, indicating the value of the concept.

Mila Elementary School: Urban		
Students: 364	Teachers: 37	
Poverty: 65%	ELL: 4%	ESE: 38%
White: 64%	African American: 15%	Hispanic: 10%
Multiracial: 8%		

Collaboration is also valued at the district level. When Cindy Westover, featured in Chapter 3, became Worthington School District's curriculum leader for reading and language arts, she found that there was not a district curriculum for reading and language arts to guide teachers. At this same time, demographic changes were taking place; students with characteristics of urban learners were moving into the suburban, high-performing district and the change was beginning to impact student-achievement data. As an example, in 2008 the district did not make Adequate Yearly Progress (AYP) with students whose first language was not English (4 percent) and with special-education students (12 percent). Cindy knew that it was important to have a framework to guide the work of the teachers and to provide support for the growing population of students who needed research-based instruction. Rather than write the framework herself or delegate the development, she created an extensive collaborative process with the district literacy leadership team (LLT). It was important for the framework for literacy to honor her predecessor, reflect the work teachers were doing, the state's expectations, and research on literacy learning. Collaboration was also implemented to assist in the development of a coherent curriculum, instruction, and assessment system. Coherence in the academic program leads to gains in student achievement (Honig & Hatch, 2004; Newmann, Smith, Allensworth, & Bryk, 2001) and relates to the guaranteed and viable curriculum noted as essential by Marzano (2003).

With her collaborative strategy, Cindy was able to accomplish more than if she only developed the guide for teachers.

The LLT is composed of a representative from primary and intermediate grades in each elementary school, and one from each middle and high school. After the LLT developed the draft framework, it was sent to each school to share with faculties and to invite feedback. Once the feedback was received and revisions were made, the framework was finalized. Then, Cindy personally went to each school to present the framework and to clarify for teachers the expectations, being sure to emphasize the curriculum alignment. Table 5.1 illustrates this progression of collaboration.

Table 5.1   Progression of Collaboration: Example

District Example	
Leader identifies need for common curriculum.	Year 1
Leader develops literacy leadership team (LLT).	
LLT develops framework for literacy.	Year 2
Leader sends framework to each school for faculty input.	
Leader revises framework.	
Leader visits each school clarifying and seeking input.	
Leader creates follow-up support: literacy loop.	Year 3
Leader creates ongoing professional development.	
Leader monitors fidelity of implementation.	Ongoing
Leader revises the structure and provides support for continuation	
School-Based Example	
Collaboration is a nonnegotiable.	Year 1
Collaboration and common language are defined.	
School priorities for collaboration are selected.	
Whole-school collaborates on what has worked and revisions needed.	Year 2
Faculty collaborates both vertically and horizontally.	
Departments collaborate on research-based instruction and literacy infusion.	Year 3
Instruction, assessment, and literacy infusion are planned collaboratively.	
Professional development occurs with book studies, action research, and study groups.	Year 4
Principal monitors collaboration by monitoring student engagement and learning in classrooms.	Ongoing

Both horizontal and vertical curriculum alignment is essential to ongoing systematic improvements (Fullan, 2006).

This collaborative process enhanced the implementation, but like any second-order change (new curricular and instructional expectations are second-order change) some teachers modeled the implementation and others needed ongoing support. To improve upon the excellent beginning in 2008, Cindy introduced the "literacy loop," a voluntary networking opportunity for all elementary teachers. They have focused discussions on goal targets, such as data-based guided reading, and provide each other with collegial coaching. As a leader in a staff position, rather than a line position, Cindy has found that positive changes in literacy learning result from professional collaboration, creation of a common language, ongoing and consistent expectations, and supportive professional development in its various forms.

Citrus County Middle Schools: Rural

Students: 3,672   Teachers: 240

Poverty: 45%   ELL: 1%   ESE: 15%

White: 84%   African   Hispanic: 5%
                American: 4%

LEADERS IN ACTION

Principals, Citrus County Middle School

> *I'm shameless. I steal from the others!*

—Mark McCoy

Citrus County Schools are on Florida's Gulf Coast and the district is considered a rural area—not a tourist destination. Because many of the students' families have long histories in the area and in the traditional Florida work of fishing and agriculture, the district is stable in its student population and in its employees. Employees are loyal to the district, have pride in the schools, and tend to remain there for their careers. The schools are continually improving and implementing research-based practices.

With this context in mind, I invited Bill Farrell, James Kusmaul, Mark McCoy, and Doug Roland to participate in the research on second-order change. I expected them to respond affirmatively, but I was surprised that the four middle school principals wanted to have the interview together—like a focus group. They share that collaboration is at the heart of their improvements; they, as a team of principals, collaborate on everything. Constantly, they learn from each other and implement each other's ideas. One might think they would be in competition, but instead they are supportive of each other's achievements. These principals believe that they are successful because of the collaborative relationships they have developed. Following are the practices they have implemented in their schools and "stolen" from each other.

The focus is on instruction. Instruction guides teacher team meetings and relates directly to the school improvement plan annually submitted to the district. After reviewing data, teachers develop their instructional plans and use research-based practices to implement them. They are expected to include literacy strategies and higher-order thinking in the instructional plans and in the implementation of instruction. Implementations are monitored with classroom walkthroughs using handheld devices to record observations. The classroom-walkthrough data is downloaded to create spreadsheets of trends that need intervention, clarification, and celebration.

In each school, the literacy program is identified as the number one priority. Each school has a literacy coach and ongoing professional development at the school. Literacy coaches collaborate and support each other's professional development. With this emphasis on literacy development, all students take reading. Principals model literacy strategies, such as read alouds, at each faculty meeting. Teachers are encouraged to earn the state endorsement in reading, along with the principals. All of the teachers, and Bill as principal at Inverness Middle School, have earned this endorsement. Chapter 6 further covers how the literacy system has been developed and implemented district wide.

Team teachers, including the reading teacher, have a common planning period for collaboration. These periods are intended for studying student data, making connections across content areas, and obtaining assistance with literacy strategies. Data days take place where leadership presents student data and the faculty draw conclusions and create steps to implement in response to the student data. Mathematics and science teachers are paired in three-hour blocks so they can be flexible in time spent in hands-on experiences and laboratory learning. This also helps teachers make interdisciplinary connections for students among content areas. Interdisciplinary teams meet with the literacy coach to incorporate literacy strategies, scaffolding students to access the content language and comprehension of difficult content text.

Because these principals have firsthand experience with how powerful collaboration can be for professional growth and deep thinking, they employ it in their schools. A different teacher from each team attends school leadership meetings each month. These principals are transparent in their collaboration with each other, and in building a culture that expects collaboration in their schools. Through their modeling of collaboration and support of collaboration, it has become the norm in their schools. Results from 2006–2008 indicate that reading, mathematics, and writing have improved under the leadership of these collaborative principals.

Legacy Middle School: Suburban

Students: 950   Teachers: 55

Poverty: 60%   ELL: 22%   ESE: 19%

White: 24%   African   Hispanic: 53%
                       American: 14%

LEADER IN ACTION

Todd Trimble, Legacy Middle School

The job is to develop teachers.

—Todd Trimble

Although Legacy Middle School is suburban, it serves diverse students. When selecting teachers to open the school, Todd made it clear that in the best interest of the students, he expected a culture of collaboration. He wanted teachers who share his passion for ensuring that all of the students receive the best education possible. In the interviews to select teachers, he listened for beliefs in making a difference in students' lives or for a sense of self-efficacy related to helping students learn.

The first year the school opened, the focus was on developing a common language around collaboration. The faculty and administrators worked at defining collaboration—what it is and what it is not. It is not meeting to talk about students who misbehave, but it is to discuss what strategies work best for classroom management or instruction to develop writing. They also determined what is important for the school's collaboration, selected priorities for collaboration, and today still work toward maintaining those priorities. The clear priority is all students being successful in learning on grade-level skills and content.

During the summer after the first year, and each summer thereafter, the faculty was invited to participate in a retreat for reflecting on the past year, and for determining revisions and focus for the upcoming year. Formal assessments, monitoring assessments, and teacher assessments were reviewed. Data from each of these was used to build a mental model of how well students learned.

Year two focused on vertical collaboration, less typical than horizontal collaboration. By vertical collaboration, Todd means that teachers who teach within the same content area (like science), but at different grade levels, meet to discuss curriculum, resources, student work, and assessments. Vertical collaboration assists the faculty in refining expectations and in defining rigor for each grade level and course. The expectations for learning are then seamless between grades.

Formal collaboration within departments was the expectation for the third year. Departments strengthened research-based instructional practice. This includes infusion of literacy strategies and supplementary instructional resources, rather than reliance on the formally adopted texts, which tend to not be written to motivate students, go deeply into concepts, nor expect high levels of thinking.

The 2008–2009 school year, and thereafter, opened with a push for collaboration across all grade levels and content areas. Teachers plan instruction and assessment together. Literacy in the content areas is the priority. Through reading, writing, and speaking with appropriate academic language and formal English, the belief is that all students will be more successful while at Legacy Middle School and in high school.

In addition to expectation for formalized collaboration, professional development workshops have been replaced with study groups and book studies. Todd encourages conversations that matter, that focus on the learning—not on the teaching. Emphasis on student learning leads to creating recovery lessons before, during, and after a unit to support all students who need additional time for learning. The expectation for the students is that they will do the work—however long it takes.

This expectation of students completing their work led to studying the concept of grading. Teachers created study groups on grading. What is to be graded? How is work to be graded? What about zeros? These study groups have resulted in teachers trying out grading practices that differ from those used in the past. Todd believes that these conversations matter, and the resulting changes in practice are in the best interest of student learning.

In contrast to some of the other leaders highlighted in this book, Todd has chosen not to require minutes or reports of the teacher collaborations. He instead engages with students to assess how well the collaboration is proceeding related to student learning. He talks to students and asks questions like, "What are you learning in ____ class? Tell me the purpose of what you are learning." This practice is consistent with his mantra to focus on the student learning, not on the teaching. Through his presence in classrooms and engagement with students, he believes he can best monitor the effect of teacher collaboration on student learning.

LEADER IN ACTION

Mike Armbruster, Ocoee High School

> *When I was a younger principal, I didn't make such difficult decisions, like nonrenewing a teacher. Now, I know my work is about the students, not the teachers.*

—Mike Armbruster

Ocoee High School: Suburban		
Students: 2,586	Teachers: 112	
Poverty: 46%	ELL: 7%	ESE: 9%
White: 38%	African American: 39%	Hispanic: 16%

Ocoee High School opened in 2004 with a faculty who had been told that the expectation of participating in PLCs was nonnegotiable. Each PLC was mandated to meet at least forty-five minutes each week. During this first year, the PLCs were charged with creating common standardized curriculum, common order of instruction, and eight common assessments. Faculty were also provided with five books to read related to the collaboration and improvement of instruction. In 2008, all faculty were given *Ahead of the Curve: The Power of Assessment to Transform Teaching and Learning* (Reeves, 2008a). At the end of the first year, 17 out of the 160 faculty transferred to another school, feeling not aligned with the culture that Mike created.

Four years later, teachers have made great strides as a result of the collaborative culture. They create common assessments and study assessment and grading. Teachers decided not to give grades below 50 percent. Mathematics teachers change grades when mastery of a concept is demonstrated. In 2007, English teachers selected writing to work on and chose a program that they all would commit to implementing. The next year, these English teachers requested professional development for mathematics, science, and social studies teachers on the incorporation of writing into their content areas.

Continual monitoring of the PLCs takes place. Minutes and notes of the meetings are monitored by the administrative team. Artifacts, such as assessments, are turned in to be reviewed. Administrators walk through classes daily to monitor for a common curriculum, instruction, assessments, and quality student work. Like any outstanding principal, Mike says that the school still has room to grow and that he continues to have concerns about the amount of lecture that takes place each day.

Are there measurable results? No faculty turnover has taken place after the first year, with the exception of loss of positions due to budget cuts. By 2007–2008, discipline referrals had been reduced by 50 percent, student tardiness to school and classes were down to only ten–fifteen each day, and in-school suspension has been eliminated due to lack of need. Most telling that the culture created through collaboration to serve students works is that Ocoee High School has gone from the highest number of suspensions and expulsions of the seventeen district high schools to the lowest. The collaborative culture has created a sense of belonging for both the faculty and students. These changes would be significant for any high school.

UCF-Progress Energy Leadership Institute:
(includes 13 diverse districts) Urban, Suburban, Rural

Students in Districts: 7,000–174,000

Total Students Represented: 750,000

LEADERS IN ACTION

UCF-Progress Energy Leadership Institute

> *This is the best professional development I have ever experienced.*

—Principal

For a five-year period, a colleague, Bill Bozeman, and I were fortunate to direct the UCF-Progress Energy Leadership Institute. This institute was made possible by a generous gift from Progress Energy to the University of Central

Florida. As the name implies, this partnership represents collaboration of a for-profit business with a nonprofit—the University of Central Florida. As we began to design the institute, we determined that thirteen district superintendents, along with ten of their principals and district administrators, would be invited to participate as district collaborative teams. Each team participated in all of the events at least for one calendar year, changing some of the team members annually for the duration of the institute.

Each session was themed around intellectual stimulation and collaboration. Before attending the institutes, the teams received books authored by the speakers and participated in a book study. The first day of each institute focused on district- and school-level applications of the target concept or theme and exemplar leadership. Cross-district activities, as well as within-district team activities, involved purposeful conversations related to the presentations. Day two began with a nationally recognized researcher—such as Michael Fullan, Doug Reeves, Rick DuFour, Bob Marzano, and Kent Peterson, to name a few. In the afternoon, participants met and had purposeful talk in job-alike groups across districts. Then they returned to their district teams to discuss applications and potential use within their schools and districts.

At the end of each calendar year, the district teams shared how the institutes had impacted leadership and learning within their schools and districts. This friendly accountability and the formal evaluations indicated that the design worked. The participants liked the strategic incorporations of experts, practitioner applications, across-district collaborations, and within-district collaborations. Book study and collaboration resulted in district implementation of the research and practices shared within the context of the institutes. Consistently, participants voiced that this model was the best professional development of their careers and led to successful implementation, because of the capacity and relationships developed.

As a closing note, a former colleague, who now works in private industry and visits schools and districts regularly, commented that she had observed something curious among a variety of districts—they incorporated the same research base to guide their district improvements, using a common language, and even using some of the same books and consultants. When I shared with her that the districts she mentioned had the same experience at our institute, she nodded, "Now I understand." When an objective observer with no prior knowledge notes the implementation of concepts, ideas, research, and results, then we know that the collaborative model is effective.

REFLECTION

Schools and districts do not make gains because of an individual teacher who teaches a few students—although those students make gain. Schools and districts make gains because every teacher uses research-based instruction in a curriculum that is aligned both horizontally and vertically. This improvement is even better if teachers look at student work together, collaborate on the level of rigor expected, and develop common assessments reflecting the rigor. Through collaboration, there is an exponential effect in the adult learning and the implementation of research-based instruction and assessment. The collaborative process is a safe vehicle for teachers to have conversations that matter and discuss controversial or emotional issues like grading. It is a safe way to try out new ideas with the support of colleagues. Collaboration should be an expectation as well as the tool for empowering teachers and leaders to grow in knowledge and expertise.

PRACTICAL TIPS

- Model the value of collaboration.
- Develop accountability for collaboration.
- Ensure that collaboration addresses data-based, student-learning needs.
- Provide structure, time, and resources for collaboration.

TRENDS IN COLLABORATION

1. Establishing collaboration as a nonnegotiable expectation.

2. Collaborating horizontally within grades or content areas and vertically across grades.

3. Using collaboration to create a coherent system of curriculum, instruction, and assessment.

4. Developing monitoring systems.

5. Holding groups accountable for collaboration.

6. Expecting measurable results.

7. Using research to support the process of collaboration and content focus.

8. Teachers leading.

9. Having conversations that matter.

10. Administrators collaborating with each other rather than competing.

11. Teachers and administrators purposefully and deliberately collaborating across schools—"super professional learning communities."

HELPFUL TERMS

Common assessments: Teacher-developed classroom, end-of-grading period, end-of-unit, or end-of-course assessments given by all who teach the same thing. Common assessments serve to equalize the level of rigor expected within a course or grade and allow comparisons of effectiveness.

Conversations that matter: Purposeful and deliberate discussions related to significant topics within a school or district. When conversations that matter are valued, then more important rather than less important, but safe, discussions take place, advancing the professional development of teachers and the learning of students.

Literacy leadership team (LLT): Team of diverse teachers and administrators whose purpose is to advance literacy learning within the school or district. The more diversity in content areas, demographics, and grades represented, the more effective the LLT will be in influencing changes in literacy learning.

Mental model: Conceptual understanding of an idea, theory, or content which is usually accompanied by a visual representation.

Professional learning community (PLC): A formalized collaborative team with common goals and accountability.

Professional collaboration: Purposeful and deliberate collaboration to find solutions to common issues, challenges, questions, or problems.

Read alouds: A fluent reader reading orally to others who do not have the text. The text should be on the grade level of the students.

Recovery lessons: Instruction to build missing background knowledge or to fill learning gaps.

Self-efficacy: Belief in oneself to accomplish what needs to take place.

Super professional learning community (super PLC): PLC that includes more than one school for a specific purpose and has a structure and support system to ensure its success.

6

Strategize for Consistency

Successful implementation of second-order changes is not accidental but strategic. As noted in Chapter 2, leaders are compelled by their commitment to all students to change the culture of the school and district, and to put organizational structures in place for effectiveness and efficiency. Intellectual growth is stimulated through various modes of professional development, illustrated in Chapter 3, to support the targeted changes. As seen in Chapter 4, the changes are so important that leaders personally lead, advocate for, and participate in all of the related experiences; they do not delegate the responsibility for the target changes. To maximize the capacity for successful implementation, leaders also create the expectation for collaboration—for themselves and those with whom they work—with accountability for results over time, as discussed in Chapter 5. All of these efforts could appear to be sporadic or disconnected if the leaders are not exceptionally strategic in creating processes and systematic follow through. This strategic process is what makes their success replicable by others in other settings. This chapter explores the extent to which the successful leaders go to ensure consistency in implementing results.

As Reeves (2006) states in describing leaders who are intentional and strategic, these leaders are not lucky. The changes do not happen by accident. Results are positive because the leaders have an understanding of what it takes to successfully implement change and create systems to do so. These systems make the replication in other schools and districts a possibility and are why readers may be able to consider some of the same strategies for their own environment. In the scenarios that follow, leaders represent the concepts of creating systems and new organizational structures as well. Then, they are followed by more examples of leaders in action.

As a successful elementary school principal appointed to lead a high school in need of improvements in student achievement, Patrick Simon of Crystal River High School is an exemplar in strategic implementation of a system to ensure success. In his words, "I had to change the school's culture from teaching students to meeting students where they were, and considering the entirety of the students." To do this, Patrick created a teacher leadership team to focus on improving instruction. This teacher leadership team is in contrast to the department chair organization found in many high schools. The roles are lead teachers for WOW/PDP (working on the work/professional development plans), lead teachers for progress monitoring, lead teachers for professional development, and professional study groups. Responsibilities for the lead teachers include budgeting, student progress monitoring, student data study, and professional development. Further detail on this organization can be found in Resource E.

Crystal River High School: Rural		
Students: 1,332	Teachers: 95	
Poverty: 34%	ELL: .4%	ESE: 21%
White: 89%	African American: 4%	Hispanic: 3%

Classroom expectations increased as teachers were expected to use research-based instruction. According to Patrick, this journey has continued. In conversations with teachers, the questions he consistently asks are:

- What does the data say?
- What did you/we do to get here?
- Now what?
- So what? (What are the conclusions and implications?)

With the expectations of *consistently* being asked these questions, faculty, staff, and administrators think more strategically and think systematically, understanding that reflection leading to improvement is expected. Supporting the expectation of improvement, all administrators conduct regular classroom walkthroughs using a district two-sided note card (5 × 8). The front of the note card has observational information and the back has boxes to check related to priorities: essential questions, vocabulary instruction, higher-order thinking, reading comprehension, data-driven instruction, reading/writing connection, and reading and writing strategies. Patrick indicates that this card is easy to use, focuses the walkthroughs, provides information for feedback, and keeps the focus of the follow-up discussions on what is important. This easy-to-use monitoring tool is represented in Resource F.

Furthermore, all teachers are responsible for students who are at risk. All teachers are on at least one student's intervention team. They mentor, coach, tutor, or even assist students with transportation to school if necessary. The message of every student being successful, and the expectation for all adults to accomplish the success, makes a difference in student learning.

At the district level, an example of staff leadership strategizing for instructional consistency in reading intervention is Jada Askew in Memphis City Schools. As a middle school reading intervention teacher, she had experienced a lack of adequate professional development for success. She felt like she was alone and on her own in learning about and in implementing the reading intervention. As a result, when she was appointed to a district-level position responsible for implementation of a middle school reading intervention, *Read 180* published by Scholastic, she created a replicable systematic process to ensure success of the teachers and greater learning gains by students. In 2008–2009, sixty teachers were involved with this professional development, teaching a total of 2,375 students in the program.

Memphis City Schools: Urban

Students: 110,000

Poverty: 90%   ELL: 5%   ESE: 15%

White: 8%   African   Hispanic: 6%
American: 86%

As a result of her experience as a reading intervention teacher and her commitment to the success of the other teachers and students, Jada created a process of systematic implementation, professional development, networking, and follow-up for reading intervention. During the summer, teachers have a two-day introduction to the reading intervention in a model classroom designed to create a mental model of the classroom expectation. After school starts, teachers review and receive additional information on how to access student data, and how to use it to make data-based instructional decisions. Jada knows that data-based instructional differentiation is at the heart of successfully intervening with below-grade-level readers. This professional development is followed up monthly with teacher networking sessions in each of the schools. The networking sessions in the schools is important so that teachers have the opportunity to visit three other teachers' classes, observe their reading intervention instruction, and take away ideas for use in one's own class. After these voluntary observations, the collegial networking begins and always includes data-based, instructional decision making and differentiation. In addition to the instructional professional development, collegial observation and coaching, and networking, the teachers are invited to take an online course for professional development in reading. For completion, they receive a one-time reward of $50, funded by the district. This small amount of money may only be symbolic, but it indicates to teachers that the learning is valuable for bringing their students' literacy learning to a deeper level.

Does the strategic and systematic approach to reading intervention implementation work? Jada indicates that the middle schools improved in reading in 2008 with 89.8 percent of sixth-grade students performing at proficient or advanced, seventh grade with 83.5 percent at proficient or advanced, and eighth grade with 88.1 percent at proficient or advanced. In 2008, if any school remained on the "needing improvement list," it was due to achievement in mathematics, not to reading.

As a consultant and researcher in literacy learning, I have found that about 50 percent of reading interventions that I have observed are implemented with consistency or fidelity to the research-based model upon which the interventions are designed. This example of a systematic process to ensure consistency in the implementation by teachers, resulting in higher student achievement, is one that many other districts could replicate or use as an example.

Creating uncommon leadership structures at the district that connect to learning at the school level is one of the trends listed at the end of this chapter. Walt Griffin, Executive Director of High Schools in Seminole County Public Schools, did just that in his line-supervisory relationship with principals. The traditional high school administrative organization is for each school-based administrator to have a responsibility related to curriculum, operations, or discipline. Since the assistant principals for curriculum often do not have experience in operations and vice versa, Walt determined that he would ask for different responsibilities, at least for the curriculum and instructional work at the district level. He now asks that each school assign a different assistant principal to literacy, mathematics, science, and social studies. When Walt or any other district leader meets with reading and writing teachers or literacy coaches, the assistant principal assigned to that responsibility also attends. Likewise, when there is a meeting for mathematics improvement or program implementation, that unique assistant principal attends. Professional development related to an innovation, such as a mathematics intervention, is attended by the assistant principal so she can support implementation with fidelity at the school. The results are that each assistant principal has become an expert in a given curriculum area and more knowledgeable about curriculum, instruction, interventions, data, and assessments for that area. Through Walt's strategic planning, he has influenced reassignment of responsibilities for knowledge and actions at the high schools on a daily basis.

Walt believes in, and is a role model for, walking the talk—strategically. Every Friday, he visits schools and classrooms. Why Friday? Well, there are two reasons. First, fewer district meetings are scheduled on Fridays so his calendar tends to be more flexible. Second, he thinks that Fridays may be the weekday for less rigorous and on-task learning in schools. By visiting classrooms on Fridays, he believes he raises the expectation for rigor and learning every day, sending a message to everyone that bell-to-bell instruction for 180 days each school year is expected.

When asked what his key to successful implementation of innovations is, Walt responds, "The key to implementing innovation is to keep a laser-like focus." His laser-like focus leads to being purposeful and deliberate, and to strategizing to systematically improve instruction. Walt is an example of district line leadership creating uncommon structures that connect to and improve learning at the school level.

Central Ridge Elementary School: Rural

Students: 704	Teachers: 50	
Poverty: 46%	ELL: 2%	ESE: 18%
White: 78%	African American: 6%	Hispanic: 8%

LEADER IN ACTION

Nancy Simon, Central Ridge Elementary School

Inspect what you expect.

—Nancy Simon

As principal of Rock Crusher Elementary School, Nancy Simon experienced great success. In 2008, 92 percent of the students met proficiency and the school made Adequate Yearly Progress (AYP). A culture had been created where excellence in teaching and continual improvement was expected. Teachers asked for book studies and created collegial study teams on their own—indicators of a school with a collaborative culture focused on teacher and student learning.

As Nancy prepared to open a new school, Central Ridge Elementary School, in the fall of 2008, she knew that she had to be strategic and detail oriented to recreate the culture focused on student learning and on continual improvement by the faculty. Students were assigned to the new Title 1 school from three other schools. To pull the students together and feel like one school, Nancy met with students and families a number of times before the new school opened. She went a step further and, in the front office area, posted artwork from the students created the previous spring in their former schools. She also had the school photographer take group pictures at each of the previous schools, merge the groups into one photograph, and showcased the new Central Ridge student body in the front office as the school opened!

Nancy found that the faculty had come from various schools and states and needed a cohesive focus, given their different backgrounds. For many of these teachers it was the first time they had worked in a Title I school. With faculty who were new to each other and a newly formed student body, Nancy was strategic in quickly setting priorities for the school's work.

To create a common language and knowledge base, the school has two conceptual foci each month, such as metacognition and schema. They also have a morning message for all teachers to write on their white boards, teach students about, and use in instruction. To achieve consistency in research-based instruction, each administrator visits classrooms daily and strategically offers comments to the teachers on the school's priorities: anchor charts, research-based instructional strategies, and essential questions. Nancy believes that the routine she has established upon entering each classroom—picking up the planning notebook and instructional journal to look for these priorities, listening and looking for them in classrooms, and following up with comments to the teachers—is essential to create consistency and a belief among the faculty that these priorities are essential.

With various skills and understanding among the faculty, Nancy understands that each faculty member is in a different place in implementing each of the priorities. She therefore has taken the classroom walk-throughs a step further than most principals might. Each Friday, Nancy sends a message to the faculty related to the week's priority—such as essential questions. Teachers respond, and share how they are using the concept and how it is helping the students learn. Nancy also visits classes and photographs teachers using the target concept. Selected photographs and comments form the *Ridgeback Reflections* to provide positive feedback and assist those who are not at high levels of implementation. The teachers' comments on the use of the concept and photographs assist other teachers in creating a mental model and clarify their understandings. An excerpt from *Ridgeback Reflections* can be found in Resource G, illustrating teacher Cathy Farrell sharing how she uses essential questions in her classroom. This attention to detail in the systematic setting of expectations for faculty and students, follow-through in implementation, feedback, and spiraling to higher levels of understanding is the core of strategizing for consistency, our current leader action theme for second-order change.

LEADER IN ACTION

Jaime Quinones, Shafter High School

> I want the teachers to buy in to literacy-based instruction. I know our students can perform better academically than they have in the past.
>
> —Jaime Quinones

Shafter High School: Urban		
Students: 1,504	Teachers: 62	
Poverty: 75%	ELL: 25%	ESE: 6%
White: 14%	African American: 1%	Hispanic: 84%

Located in an agricultural region of the state, Kern High School District is the largest high school district in California. Jaime was principal of Shafter High School for six years, and in 2008 opened Mira Monte High School, which serves the most students living in poverty in the district. At both schools, Jaime's strategy to implement second-order change has been based on maximizing the respectful relationships among the staff. This leads to increased commitment to improving literacy learning for the students. At the same time, the faculty and Jaime delved into student-achievement data to understand the degree to which the students need assistance.

This leader in action scenario will focus on the changes at Shafter High School. The teachers were frustrated because the students were not reading their assignments and participating fully in class discussions and activities. This frustration stemmed from the inability of the students to access the text and read on-grade-level text independently. No wonder the students had difficulty—about 70 percent of the students read below grade level, with the mean reading level at Grade 6 and the texts on reading levels of grades 9–12.

When the teachers engaged in studying student data with Jaime, they understood the situation more fully. Only about 26 percent of the students read on grade level and could possibly read the high school textbooks independently. Then, faculty and Jaime looked for schools within their state whose students had similar characteristics to theirs. Among them were those where students were making gains in student achievement. Jaime and the teachers visited and engaged with faculty and students in these successful schools to learn what innovations were being implemented that resulted in student-achievement gains. Together, Jaime and the faculty discovered that the high schools budgeted for a literacy coach, had professional development on literacy infusion across the content areas and grades, and committed to schoolwide independent reading. These schools strategized to support development of teachers' knowledge and skills of adolescent literacy, leading to improved student comprehension of content texts.

Following the school visits, the literacy leadership team (LLT) was developed to guide the school's literacy learning. The LLT represented teachers across the school who assisted with the implementation of schoolwide commitment to literacy infusion. Armed with a better understanding of the challenges and what might work, teachers opened to the idea of one of their own moving into the position of literacy coach, which Jaime funded out of the instructional budget. As a classroom teacher, this literacy coach had a proven track record with students who read below grade level and thus had credibility with the faculty and staff. Due to the positive relationships and credibility, the literacy coach was successful in assisting teachers with professional development, modeling in classes, instructional planning, and student assessment.

Jaime has also been strategic in developing his own knowledge of literacy and literacy leadership. He has sought opportunities to listen to experts, engage in substantive discussion, and learn as much as he can about high school literacy. He and I have had multiple conversations in this regard. He, along with his faculty, use various resources including *The K–12 Literacy Leadership Fieldbook* (Taylor & Gunter, 2006), *Literacy Coaching: A Handbook for School Leaders* (Moxley & Taylor, 2006), and *Improving Reading,*

Writing, and Content Learning (Taylor, 2007) to develop a common language and a strategic path for assisting students.

At first there were a few volunteers who wanted to change their instruction to reflect research-based literacy infusion. Jaime was happy to begin the journey of change with these volunteers and support their success. As teachers became more successful with research-based instruction, the literacy infusion practices spread.

The literacy coach began a student reading club with fifteen students; in 2008 the reading club had 150 students! The librarian sought relevant books for students that were interesting to them, making the library student friendly. Student achievement began to improve, particularly in reading. Because of the success of those who voluntarily infused literacy, the expectation for instruction at Shafter High School looks different from six years ago, and has evolved to where the school wants to be.

Jaime believes that he has to obtain teacher buy-in and commitment. He was patient but strategic in focusing the school culture on literacy learning in the daily practice. His budgetary and personnel decisions were made for what he believed to be the best interest of students' learning. Student data took the emotional and personal issues out of professional performance and focused the decision making on objective data. Professional development for himself and his faculty was targeted and collaborative. Today, he is following the same philosophy at Mira Monte High School where no doubt, student achievement will continue to improve.

LEADER IN ACTION

Tom Curry, Citrus County Schools

> *Walkthroughs by district staff say, I care about you and what you are doing.*

—Tom Curry

Citrus County Schools: Rural		
Students: 16,718		
Poverty: 45%	ELL: 1%	ESE: 20%
White: 84%	African American: 4%	Hispanic: 5%

As Lead Director for Curriculum and Instruction at Citrus County Schools, Tom Curry has an overwhelming responsibility. Due to his diligence in systematic implementation of second-order change, positive results in student achievement have been realized. He attributes successful student achievement to persistence and never giving up. His persistence has paid off. In 2008, the district was graded an A for the continued improvement of the district's schools; this was based on gains in reading, writing, and mathematics at every level—elementary, middle, and high school (see Table 6.1).

The innovation that Tom indicates as making the most difference is the literacy system initiative. It began with literacy learning by all administrators—school based and district based. With a common language and baseline knowledge of literacy learning, the district leadership opted to create and fund the literacy coach position for all schools. Once the literacy coaches were selected, Tom strategized and collaborated with the new coaches to develop their knowledge of literacy learning, adult learning, professional development, and instructional coaching. Through this process, literacy coaches collaborate to develop common professional development that is implemented in every school. Since that initial development, literacy coaches have moved to contextualized professional development much like those related to stimulating intellectual growth described in Chapter 3. The literacy coaches meet monthly as a community of learners to strategize, update each other, and plan their next steps. They support each other in the continual improvement process and assist each other with professional development in each other's schools. Furthermore, literacy resources are available to the schools and community on the district Web site, indicating the high priority of the literacy system implementation.

The research office provides various data at the district, school, and teacher level. Data relates to classroom walkthroughs, monitoring assessments, professional development, and Florida Comprehensive Assessment Test (FCAT). These various forms of data are studied to identify relationships among them. For instance, is there a relationship between the professional development in a school and gains on FCAT? Is there a relationship between walkthrough data and FCAT? (Unless someone studies and finds a relationship, then we do not know if it is a meaningful use of time.) By studying data and trends, Tom can support literacy coaches and schools in student-achievement gains with accurate, data-based information, not conjecture.

Table 6.1 Citrus County, Percent Proficient and Above (2006–2008)

Florida Comprehensive Assessment Test: Reading			
Grade	2006	2008	Percent Proficient Gain
4	76	80	4
5	74	78	4
6	66	65	−1
7	64	67	3
8	46	52	6
9	40	50	10
10	33	40	7

Beyond hard data provided by the research office, Tom spends time in schools and classrooms regularly. He conducts fidelity checks on literacy implementation two to three times a year in each classroom. At first, he said teachers were resistant to district leaders coming in their classrooms. Now, if Tom has not recently been in someone's class, a teacher will ask him why he has not been there: evidence that walkthroughs not only by school-based leaders, but also district leaders have become the norm.

Evidence of the successful implementation of literacy learning includes words walls, evidence-based vocabulary instruction, and implementation of literacy strategies at all levels. These sources of evidence are especially apparent at the high school level. District data indicates that creating a system for literacy learning has positively impacted both reading and writing; the biggest jump in test scores has been at the high school level.

REFLECTION

Consistency in implementation is the first step in measuring the impact of a second-order change. Fidelity to the research-based model being implemented is essential to measure the extent of improvement in learning yielded. Leaders who are successful at implementing change are strategic and their work is replicable because it is systematic. They carefully develop a common language with those in their schools or districts and use it consistently. Expectations are exceptionally clear, modeled, reinforced, and rewarded. Monitoring systems are put into place and used to generate data for continual improvement. Feedback is invited, modeled, and used to modify the innovation or to clarify expectations.

Think about the extent to which each of the leaders in this chapter exemplified the first six leader action themes for second-order change. Table 1.3 and Table 2.2 provide review of the themes discussed so far.

PRACTICAL TIPS

- Create and implement a timeline for strategic implementation of the target change.
- Reorganize both administrative and teacher leadership to achieve the target change.
- Systematically monitor and provide feedback on the target change.

TRENDS IN STRATEGIZING FOR CONSISTENCY

1. Regularly scheduled meetings with subordinates to ensure a common language and voice.

2. Creating *replicable systems* for implementation, feedback, monitoring, and follow-up.

3. Creating uncommon leadership and organizational systems.

4. Classrooms walkthroughs targeting priorities in instruction.

5. Monitoring with various types of data on a regular basis.

6. Connecting district leadership to school-based leadership, learning, and results.

HELPFUL TERMS

Anchor charts: Visuals that provide key terms and data for student and teacher support.

Data-based instructional differentiation: Differentiating instruction for individuals or groups of students using ongoing student data as the basis for the decision making.

Essential questions: Big idea or concept stated as a question of the learning target.

Fidelity: Implementation according to the research base of the product, procedure, or concept.

Independent reading: Students reading books of their own choice on their independent reading level (reading without teacher support).

Metacognition: Thinking about one's thinking; understanding one's own learning.

Professional development plan (PDP): Required for teacher to write in some school districts, usually related to data-based goals of the school.

Schema: Background knowledge upon which to build new learning.

Word walls: Vocabulary strategy where words, definitions, examples, and visuals may be posted.

Working on the work (WOW): Focused actions directed at specific school target goals (work).

7

Let the Data Speak

Then Take Action

Data means different things in different school levels and locations. In some settings, it only means end of the year, formal assessment data—which is woefully inadequate since it is one point in an entire school year. In other settings, data means student work—observational data and monitoring ongoing data in mathematics and science, attendance, and discipline. In some examples used in this book, data refers to records gathered from various sources: classroom observations and walkthroughs including the level of thinking teachers have in the student work, level of questions, numbers of students engaged, or number of students achieving benchmark levels in instruction. In schools and districts not continually improving in student achievement, I have noticed a lack of ongoing monitoring data for both students and teachers. The patterns indicate little to no study of student data at the teacher level, and these schools attribute achievement results to student characteristics, not to the work of the adults. As an example, consider a high-performing, high-socioeconomic district that *did not* make Adequate Yearly Progress (AYP) in 2007 or 2008 due to lack of performance by subgroups. One respected educator who works in this district took me aback with this remark, "What do you expect? Those students don't have the ability to learn any better! That is why we don't make AYP."

Students and adults rise or lower themselves to the expectation given them. In schools and districts making consistent growth, implementing useful data management systems evidences commitment to all students improving. This includes monitoring data and classroom data so there are no surprises when the formal assessment data arrives.

In some states, the summative accountability data is the driving force for the school and district. This data may or may not be aligned with national data sources, such as National Assessment of Educational Progress (NAEP). Deep-thinking leaders question how to move the schools beyond the state accountability since proficiency is set by the state and may be below grade level nationally when compared with NAEP. Such leaders are wise to implement other assessments for monitoring achievement within the school year and for identifying students needing intervention. They also incorporate student work in data study to assist teachers in thinking about instruction and the quality of student products generated as a result.

Other leaders, like those highlighted in each chapter, use various forms of data to determine direction for the school or district, to determine which students need which services, and to determine which faculty are most effective with which students. They also use data to allocate scarce resources across a school district and within a school. Data can effectively drive personnel decisions as well as student decisions. Most importantly, the leaders whose schools successfully make second-order change take data analysis to the teacher level. Then, they expect teachers to make data-based instructional decisions. The examples in this text illustrate this with both school-based principals and with district leaders.

Data study linked to data-based decisions is essential. If decisions are not made based on data, then they will be based on personal experience perhaps as a learner, or on folk stories, or for adult convenience (Reeves, 2008a), just like the example in the opening paragraph. Data days, like those in Chapter 2 with Paula St. Francis, and Citrus County middle school principals in Chapter 5, focus where it can make a difference in student learning. These examples represent second-order change for those who use data-based decision making and for each of the scenarios that follow.

Dale Moxley (Chapter 3) indicated that the students were doing well, but not getting better. There was no sense of urgency. With the assistance of the curriculum resource teacher, literacy coach, and data coach, a data walkthrough has been created. Grade levels now spread out their data along with assessments and examples of student work. Cross-grade-level teams walk through each of the grade-level displays and have discussions about all three artifacts at each grade level, providing feedback and new perspectives to the teachers. As a result of this type of data analysis, teachers can align their instruction and level of rigor vertically and not just horizontally. As an example, what does third-grade work look like to the second-grade teacher? The fourth-grade teacher? Is it less rigorous in third than second? To the fourth-grade teacher, does it look challenging or too easy? This experience has led to changes in writing instruction and positive gains in writing results in particular. Alignment of curriculum horizontally and vertically is important to higher levels of student achievement, and data study can assist with accomplishing this alignment.

"Imagine, believe, achieve" is the mantra at Castle Creek Elementary School. Joy Taylor led with those words in mind when she designed the data-based decision-making and monitoring system. Although the school is suburban, the poverty level is high and there are many students with learning needs. Data

Castle Creek Elementary School: Suburban		
Students: 720	Teachers: 50	
Poverty: 57%	ELL: 25%	ESE: 14%
White: 42%	African American: 8%	Hispanic: 50%

meetings are held weekly with teachers to monitor Dynamic Indicators of Basic Early Literacy Skills (DIBELS) for students in Grades K–5 who receive intensive reading instruction. For other students, the monitoring is every other week.

Joy expects the teachers to plan together and learn from each other. As grade-level teams, they study student data and plan to differentiate instruction together, resulting in regrouping *across the grade* for more explicit, data-based differentiation in instruction. Regrouping across the grade, rather than within the classroom, assists the teachers in focusing on a smaller number of groups. Joy believes that having more grouping levels supports students with more specific differentiation of instruction. These are flexible groups that vary with achievement of skills and knowledge throughout the school year.

Quality of instruction is the expectation, not quantity of instruction. The expectation of quality instruction is why the classroom teacher works with intervention students, while other adults, perhaps paraprofessionals or teachers, instruct nonintervention students during that particular portion of class time. Joy has found that there are teachers who are successful with one type of student yet when asked to teach a different type of student, they may need support. (Nancy Simon found the same thing as she opened the new elementary school.) Joy's expectations based on individual student data are clear, "I expect students to actually be engaged in learning, not just doing an assignment." Using data-based decision making for differentiation in instruction yields her a coveted recognition. She is a principal whose students exceed the district researchers' prediction for achievement based on previous performance and demographic variables.

Unlike leaders in districts or schools under watch or on an improvement list of their state or district, leaders of high-performing schools often have a difficult time creating a sense of urgency for change. Beth Thedy, former principal of Suntree Elementary School, shares that this was a frustration for her in that assignment. While the school was high performing, all students were not high performing. In our communication, Beth referred to Schmoker (2006), "[. . .] schools, like any effective organization, will need to be tougher, clearer, and uncompromising when essential, reasonable expectations are not met" (p. 145). (Remember that these successful principals know the research and literature and offer it without being asked?) Taking Schmoker's words to heart, Beth began to have difficult conversations with individual teachers based on the achievement data of the students they taught. Frequently, those who believed they were high performing and perceived to be high performing did not have the most gains in student achievement when compared to other teachers. Some teachers even got emotional or tearful when confronted with their students' data. Reponses would be something like, "It's the kids!" Individual teacher data meetings were followed with team data meetings. Facing the data on every student, with the expectation that every student would improve, created the sense of urgency needed among the teachers. No longer could they be happy that the school as a whole was high performing or that as individual teachers they were perceived to be excellent—now excellence would be measured in all students learning more.

Professional development goals for faculty were adjusted to reflect the newly found motivation that emerged from understanding the student data, and also the expectations that went along with the data. When the AYP data came out for that school year, the faculty celebrated the improvement in every subgroup—including those students served by special education or by the English as a Second Language program. No longer did the teachers blame students for the data. Teachers' conversations changed from referring to the students as the cause for lack of achievement to their instruction as the cause for gains in student achievement.

Lewisburg K–8 School: Rural		
Students: 599	Teachers: 40	
Poverty: 58%	ELL: 1%	ESE: 39%
White: 98%	African American: 1%	Hispanic: 1%

LEADER IN ACTION

Barrett Nelson, Lewisburg K–8 School

> *We're not where we were, and not where we need to be.*
>
> —Barrett Nelson

Barrett Nelson has accomplished a great deal for the students he serves. He came to Lewisburg with experience as a high school assistant principal in another district. Initially, the faculty was wary of him since he was not from their stable rural community, nor from an elementary school background. In his understated way, he told the faculty and staff that he had a lot to learn about elementary school and particularly about the primary grades (prekindergarten through third grades). He committed himself to becoming knowledgeable of elementary school research, its teachers, curriculum, instruction, resources, and assessment.

Lewisburg serves the lowest socioeconomic area of the county and, of the five elementary schools, had the lowest student achievement in 2004. Barrett, like many other leaders in this text, knew he had to raise the expectations for student learning and not allow the economic level of the community nor past student achievement influence the expectations. This meant the expectations for the adults had to increase also. The school would no longer continue as status quo.

First, a core reading series was implemented in kindergarten–sixth grade to bring consistency in expectations for resources, curriculum, instruction, and what "on grade-level" student work looked like. This was a huge adjustment for the teachers as they were accustomed to using the instructional resources of their choice with no pressure to improve learning. Some did not expect the students to achieve at high levels. Along with the core reading series came intensive reading intervention for readers who are at risk in kindergarten–third grade, and in 2007, intensive reading intervention for below-level readers in fourth–eighth grade.

A strategy to begin the necessary collaboration for addressing learning needs was to start with environmental walkthroughs. This was an after-school professional development experience where the faculty walked through each other's classrooms, making notes of exemplary literacy-rich and well-organized classrooms. These representations appeared to have the elements of reading (phonics, phonemic awareness, vocabulary, fluency, comprehension). The purpose was to create a mental model of a literacy-rich classroom modeling research-based instruction. Following the environmental walkthroughs, teachers discussed what they saw and what they liked, and changes they would make in their own rooms. Preparing the classroom environment to facilitate learning and to represent research-based instruction was a safe first step.

Today, collaboration at Lewisburg has grown beyond the environmental walkthroughs. Grades and teams study student data on an ongoing basis. Student work is shared and teachers use it to assist each other in being more effective with each student. They write plans for individual students to improve their learning. Data study of individual students and taking action on that data is essential to continue the achievement growth. Barrett participates in these sessions with the teachers, demonstrating how important it is to focus on each student's progress, work, and strategies for success. He does not delegate the leadership for changing student achievement.

Furthermore, each grade or team plans instruction and assessment together. In sharing student work, they discuss rigor and the expectations that students should achieve. This is particularly important since teachers may have had low expectations for the students based on historical perceptions of performance. To optimize the collaboration, the curriculum has been aligned both horizontally within a grade and vertically grade to grade; this provides a seamless learning experience for students.

Under Barrett's leadership, the students have made amazing gains in achievement according to DIBELS and Group Reading and Diagnostic Assessment (GRADE). By 2008, the school had achieved similarly to its higher socioeconomic counterparts. In some grade levels, Lewisburg students achieved higher than the other elementary schools in the district. Using data to guide decision making, along with higher expectations and a culture focusing on what is best for students, has yielded measureable results.

Crooms Academy of Information Technology: Urban

Students: 592   Teachers: 38

Poverty: 33%   ELL: 3%   ESE: 13%

White: 50%   African   Hispanic: 22%
                American: 20%

Multiracial: 5%   Asian: 3%

LEADER IN ACTION

Connie Collins, Crooms Academy of Information Technology

> *We're closing the achievement gap. We do what it takes for each individual student.*

—Connie Collins

Crooms Academy of Information Technology is a high school of choice, located in a low-socioeconomic community. As a school of choice, students come from throughout the district, but many also come from the community where the school is located. The administration and faculty are committed to doing whatever it takes for every student to succeed.

Ongoing data monitoring is a process that guides decision making for the faculty and administration. Students are progress monitored in reading, writing, mathematics, and science—more extensive monitoring than most high school students experience. Students who are assessed as below proficient in any area have an academic advocate responsible for monitoring and directing the student to assistance as needed. "Academic advocate" is the term assigned, rather than mentor, since these teachers and administrators attend teacher conferences with the students, go to bat for them when necessary, and assist them any way that a well-educated parent might do.

Students are expected to own their achievement data. All students are responsible for having in the Florida Comprehensive Achievement Test strand results from the previous spring in their notebooks. Rather than saying, "I have to work on mathematics," a student with specific strand performance known will say, "I have to work on the strand of geometry or algebraic reasoning." Monitoring data in reading, writing, and mathematics are also maintained in the notebooks so students can track their progress toward making gains before the annual summative assessment. By having ownership of their own data, they are empowered to make positive decisions about changing their own results. Weekly tutoring sessions are held on FCAT strands and students are expected to attend tutoring when their strand of need is the focus of tutoring. The student ownership also ensures that FCAT is not something done to them or threatening them, rather it has become a part of school that they have some control over; it is not a mystery. For high school students, this is a conceptual shift in thinking about high-stakes accountability assessment.

Connie carefully attends to the lowest 30 percent of the students with strategic scheduling decisions. Students who are below proficient in mathematics have a double block for mathematics. Students who score below proficient in reading and do not do well on an oral reading fluency test in August are assigned to a double block for reading, plus a language arts class. Students who score near proficient are assigned a single block of reading in addition to a language arts class. Literacy strategies and technology are integrated throughout all content classes to support students' success across content areas.

Connie and the leadership team continue to study student data and ask, "What else can we do for our lower-achieving students?" From this, a promising idea has emerged. Since the lowest-achieving students are also living in poverty and have little experience beyond the neighborhood, the assistant principal designed and sponsors the Explorer's Club for them. The purpose of the Explorer's Club is to provide cultural experiences and related instruction outside of the school day, at no charge to the students. These students attend plays; go to history, art and science centers; and to other events that they may not otherwise experience. Before each of the events, students prepare during afterschool sessions to gain background knowledge and appropriate academic vocabulary. After the event, the students debrief on what they learned and what else they would like to know.

Connie believes that the combination of these data-based decisions is why the FCAT scores and other measures have continued to increase during the school's seven-year history. In 2008, Crooms had a 100-percent graduation rate. Hispanic, African American, and students receiving free- or reduced-price lunch benefits scored at the same level in writing as their nonminority, higher socioeconomic counterparts. Also in 2008, the achievement gap was closing in reading, mathematics, and science. Connie's dedication to all students learning more earned her the National Association of Secondary School Principals Florida principal of the year award for 2009.

LEADER IN ACTION

Van Mitchell, Colonial High School

> *Our teachers use more data to make instructional decisions than any other school.*

—Van Mitchell

Colonial High School: Urban		
Students: 3,800	Teachers: 184	
Poverty: 55%	ELL: 28%	ESE: 21%
White: 34%	African American: 9%	Hispanic: 64%

Van Mitchell is known to be a successful principal with a challenging student population. Van was even acknowledged by the National Association of Secondary Principals as a finalist for national high school principal of the year. Colonial High School consistently outperforms the projections made for student scores on accountability assessments based on demographic characteristics, such as poverty, mobility, and academic achievement before entering the school. (Only 33 percent enter the high school reading at the proficient level.) In fact, Colonial High School students made the greatest gains in reading and writing of any of the seventeen high schools in the school district in 2008.

It is clear that Van speaks from a data-research perspective when he discusses the multiple strategic approaches that go on at his school every day—from literacy infusion, to common classroom assessments, to an instructional calendar, to writing twice each week in every class. Turning to two computer monitors, Van brings up different data sources. One screen has summative data and school data. The other is a Web-based program developed by the personnel in the school. This Web-based program has many data sources: standardized achievement; monitoring assessment; attendance; teacher comments; and up-to-date, teacher-given grades. Van easily clicks on a list of students who were low performing in the ninth grade and goes to their individual tenth-grade data; in addition to standardized assessment and monitoring data, this includes up-to-date, teacher-given grades; teacher comments; and class attendance. Van tells how individual students are progressing in their daily work—not just how the students performed on the previous spring's assessment.

Van also links to a teacher's page and shows the same information for a given class. Teachers have their students' data easily available. They are expected to intervene or seek support when necessary based on classroom-performance data.

This is a transparent system and highly responsive. Through the use of the Web-based data-management system, teachers, administrators, and counselors monitor all students who are at risk of not being successful. As an example, Van demonstrates a search for all students with a GPA 2.0 or lower. Then, Van checks their current work, after which he e-mails teachers regarding the student's progress or lack of progress. This is a major effort that is ongoing on a daily basis, but it pays off.

The system is also helpful when engaging with families of the students. When school representatives meet with parents, they quickly access the student's data and share up-to-date information with parents. Parents are often surprised at the detail and the amount of the data. They also may be surprised by their student's absences, lack of homework completion, or any of the other pertinent information. Frequently, the student's version of his performance is not consistent with the data shared with the parents. This system provides an objective way to engage the parents in deeper understanding of their student's learning, leading to a discussion of how to support more success.

Student data is not the only data maintained. Van understands that the aligned curriculum, research-based instruction, infusion of literacy and reading benchmarks throughout the curriculum, and common assessments are essential first steps for improving student achievement. With this understanding in mind, he monitors data from classroom walkthroughs by the administrative team (seven assistant principals) and himself. He and the administrative team conducted 1,644 classroom walkthroughs in the 2007–2008 school year. During these walkthroughs, they looked for curriculum alignment, high engagement in learning by students, higher-order questions and student work, and posted learning goals for the day's instruction. In all of the classroom walkthroughs during 2007–2008, only twenty-two times were the learning goals not posted.

Twenty-two is not significant; what is significant is that the leadership maintains data on learning priorities and knows, with certainty, who emphasizes the data, who does not, and how often.

The leader action theme for second order-change, "Let the data speak, then take action," is modeled daily at Colonial High School. As Van says, "We are better than we were, not as excellent as we need to be." Making decisions for each individual student at the teacher level, and monitoring with various data sources at the leadership level, makes a difference in student achievement.

LEADER IN ACTION

Anna Marie Cote, Seminole County Public Schools

Data drives everything in the district, beginning with the budget.

—Anna Marie Cote

Seminole County Public Schools: Suburban

Students: 65,299 Poverty: 34%

ELL: 16%   ESE: 15%

White: 58%   African   Hispanic: 18%
                 American: 13%

Asian: 4%   Other: 7%

Data use at the district level is more than predicting which schools will make AYP. According to Anna Marie Cote, Deputy Superintendent in Seminole County Schools, data drives all decisions. She emphasizes that the administrators at the district and at the schools are a team, working together for each student's success. (The principals echo this team culture between the district and schools.) The superintendent invites authentic feedback and ideas so that the district continues to increase student achievement. He has been known to say, "Tell me what I need to know, not what you think I want to hear." All administrators are focused on each student learning as much as possible.

District budget meetings for the following year begin each October. They begin, not with what each department needs (transportation, facilities, instruction, operations, etc.), but with student-achievement data. From careful analysis of the data, the budget committee moves to a root-cause analysis. Anna Marie indicated that through determining the root cause, they are able to generate viable solutions to challenges. Once the priorities for the district are determined, then the budgeting decisions can be aligned with priorities. An example is prioritizing funds for curriculum alignment (lack of alignment being identified as a root cause) to assist with reducing the achievement gaps.

With student-achievement data driving the budget, decisions are made to assist individual schools (see Table 7.1). As a result, some schools receive funds differently than other schools, depending upon the students' needs. This assistance means that some other important projects might not be implemented. This budget process supports both district- and school-level leaders in not swaying from what has been identified as most

Table 7.1 Comparison of Data-Based Decision Making: Schools With and Without Consistent Growth in Student Achievement

Consistent Growth in Student Achievement	Lack of Consistent Growth in Student Achievement	Notes What do we need to do?
Summative data is one of several pieces of evidence studied.	Only summative data is studied.	
Data-based instructional planning is expected and inspected.	Data-based instructional planning is expected and encouraged.	
Monitoring data guides instructional planning, differentiation, and intervention.	Monitoring data may not be available.	
Monitoring data includes student work for on-grade-level performance and rigor.	Student work may not be studied for on-grade-level expectations or rigor.	
Data-management systems are easily accessible by faculty, administrators, and parents.	Data-management systems may be cumbersome to access or not available.	
Data is available in real time and is up to date.	Data may be out of date when it becomes available.	
Data drives innovation for all students.	Data drives innovation for lowest performers.	
Teachers intervene with students.	Noncertified personnel intervene with students.	
Data creates a sense of urgency for change.	Data confirms student abilities and background.	
Students own their data.	Data is a mystery to students.	
Student-achievement data drives budget decisions.	Budget decisions are driven by needs other than student achievement.	

important. It also helps maintain a financial as well as academic focus based on student-achievement data.

The clear communications, openness to authentic feedback, and use of data-based decision making works. The state has identified Seminole County Schools as one of ten high-performing districts out of sixty-seven. It has the highest percent of the budget directly used in classrooms in the state—65 percent. Seminole County Schools consistently improves in reading, writing, and mathematics performance, at all levels.

REFLECTION

In this time of accountability, leaders cannot afford personal opinion or educational folklore to guide leadership decisions. Developing and incorporating real-time student-data management systems, and their systematic use, can support data-based decision making by parents, students, teachers, and leaders. Most recently, many school districts have encountered budget shortfalls reflecting the economic challenges of our communities. Data-based decision making assists in objectivity with financial decisions, as well as with personnel and instructional decisions. Using data to make decisions is essential for every student to achieve at the highest possible level.

PRACTICAL TIPS

- Regularly schedule time with teachers to study their student data, and assist with instructional decisions based on that data.
- Implement a data-management system that is easy to use.
- Ask:
  o "Who is learning and who is not learning?"
  o "What data are you using to make these decisions?"
  o "What are you going to do about it?"
  o "How will you know if the learning improves?"

- Implement a monitoring-assessment system for at least those reading and performing in mathematics below the fiftieth percentile nationally.

TRENDS IN DATA-BASED DECISION MAKING

1. Using multiple data sources: observational, behavioral, student work, monitoring, formative, and summative.

2. Using student-achievement data to drive the budget development process.

3. Exceeding predictions of student achievement based on demographics and past performance.

4. Closing the achievement gap by targeting individuals.

5. Expecting students to own their data.

6. Using data and student work to align the curriculum horizontally and vertically.

7. Creating a system for easy access to student classroom data.

8. Leveraging the objectivity of data to create a sense of urgency for second-order change.

HELPFUL TERMS

Academic advocate: An adult in the school who mentors, supports, speaks up for, and represents students just as a parent might.

Adequate Yearly Progress (AYP): Academic progress according to No Child Left Behind, including specific subgroups.

Differentiated instruction: Varying instruction for individuals and groups of students, based on data.

Engage in learning: Students understanding what they are doing, why they are doing it, how to measure the results, how to do it correctly, and how to explain it.

Environmental walkthrough: Classroom walkthrough focused on specific physical/organizational elements of the classroom that reflect research-based instruction.

Formative assessment: Assessment given to determine what a student has learned and what a student still needs to learn.

Intensive reading intervention: Curriculum, instruction, resources, and assessment intended to improve a student's performance.

Monitoring data: Data for monitoring progress or learning within the school year that supports making changes that same year. It may have a relationship to the formal accountability assessment.

Regrouping: Data-based grouping and then grouping differently for other purposes or based on new data.

Summative assessment: Assessment at the end of a unit of learning.

8

Engage Families in Learning

Inherently, we know that engaging families in the school has a high value, but we may take it for granted that those who are interested participate and support the school at home, while those who are not interested, or do not have the skills to help their children in furthering their learning, do not. This theme was not built into any of the interview questions used as a basis for this book, nor did any of the background research target families. However, leaders pointed to strategic family engagement as one of the second-order changes they led or targeted family engagement as a significant reason why they believe their student achievement increased. As a result, this leader action theme for second-order change emerged. Leaders continually indicate how essential engaging the families is to the successful implementation of the change. The largest percentage of leaders indicating that engaging families was essential was at the elementary and high school levels.

It is possible that other leaders engage families in the learning process, but they did not explicitly identify these actions during the interview. Certainly, the leaders who did not identify family engagement recognize its value, but may take it for granted or not attribute the positive changes in their student achievement to this variable.

The relationship between parental and family involvement in school and student achievement has wide support (Allen, 2008; Glickman, 2002; Henderson & Mapp, 2002; Reeves, 2004). In leadership experiences and in previous writing, I have strategized to engage parents and caregivers in substantive ways, such as family literacy or mathematics evenings (Taylor & Gunter, 2006; Taylor, 2007). Substantive parental or family involvement does not mean membership in the parent organization, but involvement in the learning. It is this involvement that makes the difference in student achievement (Allen, 2008). Although this relationship is generally accepted, principals and leadership indicated that they know the need to engage the parents, but it is the last goal on the list and they just may not get to it.

Findings from this particular research suggest that the traditional expectations of parental/caregiver involvement in a student's education or participation in parent groups, like school advisory councils, is not enough. It is at least not enough to support implementation of second-order change in a school for gains in student achievement. When schools or districts feel a sense of urgency to make significant change, they then may develop substantive educative experiences for families so that the results from the target change continue to grow over time. In contrast to data-based instruction, which focuses on each individual student, engaging families in the learning process is broader and seeks to educate all members of the family or even a community. Data-based instruction and engagement of families in the learning process together create an accountability system for everyone involved.

Carol Kelley, principal of New Smyrna Beach High School, shares easy-to-implement and practical examples of family-engagement outreach. Teachers each send two postcards to homes of students who are failing, but whom they believe can be assisted in passing. On the postcard, each teacher expresses this positive belief and what each is willing to do to ensure success of the student. Response has been overwhelmingly positive as many students have never received any U.S. mail and certainly their families are not used to such outreach. One parent of a special-education student called the principal, crying, and expressed that in none of the previous nine years of school had she been communicated with in such a positive manner, and that as a parent, she would do whatever it would take to make the success happen! Other feedback has been subtler, such as a student speaking in class who has never said anything before, or just saying good morning to a teacher rather than looking down. For high school students who have not found success in school, changes in their approach to teachers and confidence—like speaking to the teacher—are positive steps.

In reflecting on what these leaders share, it makes a lot of sense. Many families, whose students attend schools with a sense of urgency to improve student achievement, have more than one child. These children grow up and soon have students in school themselves. By engaging the family in learning, the immediate need for improvement in student achievement is addressed for students, as well as the long-range need of continual improvement.

Leaders in action represented in this chapter could easily be cited as positive role models in the other chapters, and some are. Since these leaders are explicit in expressing a belief that their family-engagement efforts relate to student successes, they are represented here. Examples of substantive engagement of families in the learning process follow, representing both principals and district-level leadership. These scenarios are shared in the context of the second-order changes they have brought about.

LEADER IN ACTION

Gonzalo La Cava, Oakshire Elementary School

> *Our teachers and students must be proficient in English and in their home language.*

—Gonzalo La Cava

Oakshire Elementary School: Suburban		
Students: 744	Teachers: 51	
Poverty: 77%	ELL: 52%	ESE: 13%
White: 8%	African American: 7%	Hispanic: 78%

Gonzalo La Cava assumed the principal position at Oakshire Elementary School in 2005. This is his first principal appointment. Although Oakshire is categorized as suburban, 77 percent of the students receive free-or reduced-price lunch benefits.

Because of the large population of students whose primary home language is not English, the delivery model of instruction is one-way, developmental bilingual. Gonzalo defines this approach as one that assists language-enriched students to develop cognitive skills in their primary home language that will gradually transfer into English at a level where they can be successful in an English-only classroom. The expectation is that students are to become proficient in both their home language and English.

During his tenure, Gonzalo has focused on fidelity to the one-way bilingual model. To do this, he has made organizational changes and personnel changes. He attributes having authentic and difficult conversations with faculty and paraprofessionals for part of the success of the school. All employees must be proficient in both Spanish and English—which in itself can be a challenge. The one-way bilingual model has the expectation that content instruction will be on grade level in both the home language and in English. In practice, this means that a student may have mathematics or science twice in one day—once in English and once in Spanish. The content curriculum is not at the proficiency level of the student's English; it is instead at the student's grade level, ensuring that the student's content learning is not delayed while acquiring English proficiency. This is a critical distinction from experiences students may have in other schools.

Most pointedly to this theme, Gonzalo realizes that he is serving families. In his discussions with families, one of the tasks is to educate them on the one-way bilingual program and what it means for student expectations. He shares with families how they can facilitate the philosophical model at home. According to Gonzalo, many families are surprised to learn that their students should continue to speak their primary home language while becoming proficient in English. Some parents have been so concerned about their children being successful in English that they previously had prevented the children from using the primary home language.

To support the one-way bilingual model, the teachers offer English for adult learners. Since many of the adults in the homes lack English proficiency, the students improve as their families improve. This strategy, coupled with learning about the expectations of one-way bilingual instruction, has boosted parental involvement and has boosted gains in student achievement.

Engaging families in learning about the instructional model and philosophy, as well the adults' acquisition of English proficiency, support the increases in student achievement realized. In 2008, 70 percent of the students at Oakshire Elementary School made learning gains and the school achieved Adequate Yearly Progress (AYP).

Leesburg High School: Small town/rural		
Students: 1,700	Teachers: 108	
Poverty: 39%	ELL: less than 1%	ESE: 25%
White: 64%	African American: 35%	Hispanic: 1%

LEADER IN ACTION

Nancy Velez, Leesburg High School

Every single teacher is responsible for the achievement of every student.

—Nancy Velez

Four years ago, before being appointed principal of Leesburg High School in rural Central Florida, Nancy Velez was acknowledged as a successful principal at her previous school. She was so successful that the community of the former school protested at the school board meeting when she was transferred, but her knowledge and leadership skills were needed more at the new assignment.

The combination of poverty and a large percent of the students with identified disabilities create a challenge for raising student achievement at the high school level. As Nancy studied the student-achievement data, and shared it with the faculty, they learned that only 18 percent of the students were reaching the proficient level on the Florida Comprehensive Achievement Test (FCAT). Many of those were not excelling in classwork and could do better.

As the culture and philosophy of the school changed, making every teacher responsible for every student, the expectations for faculty were raised. By offering both honors (college preparatory) and Advance Placement (AP) courses for the students perceived as achieving, these courses served to segregate the "have students" from the "have-not students." To remedy this practice, honors classes were eliminated so that all students would be heterogeneously grouped in courses together, with higher expectations collectively, or students would be in AP classes with a new philosophy of inclusion, rather than exclusion. The new inclusion philosophy eliminated strict prerequisites for enrollment and allowed students who were willing to work hard to enroll, despite an academic or workload challenge.

Professional development of each teacher is now a high priority and the school has an extensive offering of sessions related to technology integration, literacy, and content curriculum enhancement. All English teachers are required to become endorsed or certified in reading and all other teachers are required to become endorsed in content-area reading. This requirement by Nancy has not been questioned by newly hired teachers and has served to support literacy growth in every classroom.

Instructional plans reflect the professional development with at least three instructional components: literacy strategies, technology integration, and support for students whose primary home language is not English and for special-education students. Each teacher has individual data and plans for each student taught—even in AP classes.

With these changes as a context—since a leader can only control what goes on within the school day—Nancy knew to maximize gains in student achievement the families had to be engaged. One of the first issues the families needed to assist with was deplorable student absenteeism—26 percent. Nancy implemented an attendance policy where a student can receive three excused absences with a parental note. After three, each absence has to have a physician's note. Along with this change, incentives—such as points added to semester exams for few absences and disincentives for more than four unexcused absences—serve to motivate improved attendance. In contrast to prior practice, no preferential treatment is given to empowered families. Once the students accepted the incentives to have improved attendance, they were at school more and naturally the students learned more. In fact, not too many students' grade point averages actually changed, but being in school more has changed achievement. Mixing attendance and student grades is controversial, but it has worked at Leesburg High School. In fact, this policy has been so successful that other high schools in the district have adopted it. Readers interested in this policy will find excerpts in Resource H.

Participation in family activities provided by Leesburg High School was also low when Nancy became the principal. Typically, about 25 parents out of 1,700 attended any type of open house or parent meeting. To increase this number, faculty were asked to personally call each student's family and invite them to attend parent events. Over 300 parents attended open house in fall of 2008 as a result of the personal outreach—not a computer call. For some schools, this number of parents may not seem significant, but for Leesburg the improvement is twelve times the baseline data.

To further engage the families, they have been given access to each teacher's syllabi on the school Web site. They can check their own child's attendance, grades, and missing work. Accountability for the parents to check on their own students and address school participation and performance at home is an enormous step. No longer can parents say that they are not familiar with their student's performance.

What results have been yielded in the first four years of Nancy's leadership? One of the observed changes is teachers' use of more research-based instruction, more volunteers attending professional development outside of the school day, and increased support for student learning beyond the school day. Data also support that the second-order changes are working—the number of students in reading intervention classes has been reduced due to their improved reading scores. The 32 percent of the students scoring proficient on FCAT reading grew to 44 percent the first year of her leadership. The dropout rate reduced from 6.7 percent to 2.9 percent between 2004–2008. And the student absentee rate dropped from 26 percent to 11.8 percent in 2008. This data speaks for itself, but there is still more work to be done.

As in other schools noted in this book, change often requires difficult conversations with faculty and it is no different at Leesburg High School. During the first four years, 69 percent of the faculty changed, but beginning the fifth year, there were no changes. With stability of the faculty, expectations for every teacher to be responsible for every student's achievement, and parental engagement, the student achievement is expected to continue to improve.

South Cobb High School: Urban		
Students: 2,445	Teachers: 160	
Poverty: 40%	ELL: 3%	ESE: 12%
White: 27%	African American: 58%	Hispanic: 10%
Asian: 2%		

LEADER IN ACTION

Grant Rivera, South Cobb High School

> *We didn't involve parents; we engaged families in the success of their students.*

—Grant Rivera

South Cobb High School has had a history of mediocre student achievement and there has been a perception among many—at the school and in the community—that this would not change. The first year Grant Rivera was principal, the school was in its first year of corrective action by the Department of Education. Accountability in Georgia for No Child Left Behind rests with the eleventh-grade assessment, so this is the initial grade level Grant targeted for change. This strategy contrasts to beginning with ninth grade, then moving to tenth grade, and then to eleventh grade, which nationally is more common.

In the first year, the curriculum was aligned with the state standards and benchmarks. Integrated mathematics (general/applied mathematics) was eliminated and all students began to take the higher-level course, algebra. Expectations for teachers' collaborative planning along with data study were implemented. Tight measures of accountability were added related to mastery of benchmarks. Difficult conversations took place with faculty, as the status quo for teaching and student performance was no longer acceptable. The conversations related to changes in expectations and accountability for student learning resulted in high teacher turnover the first year, just as other principals in this book experienced.

Through his leadership and the team effort of everyone in the school, the school achieved AYP for each of the following two years and all subgroups made gains. It is important to emphasize that many high schools in the school district, whose students are more economically advantaged than at South Cobb, did not make AYP. The focus of the leadership became success on their accountability assessment—the Georgia High School Graduation Test (GHSGT). It would be typical for most schools to focus on their accountability assessment. What is atypical is the extent to which faculty and administrators at South Cobb communicated with the families to accelerate the improvements.

This process of communication begins with each at-risk student's data analyzed to develop a profile. The profile includes performance on practice tests and anecdotal evidence. Once the profile is developed, it is communicated to the student's teachers, but also *to the families*. Teachers are held accountable for supporting the student's academic development, and tutoring the students if needed. If students do not show for tutoring, their families are called so that students will be present at the next day's session.

Since the student's profile is shared with the family, they develop an understanding of the student's strengths and weakness at a deeper level than previously. They also participate in developing a plan for the student to achieve success so they feel part of the process. The plan may include after-school tutoring that targets skills in six-week sessions. It may also include what families can do at home. One question that arises for underperforming students is, "Do families have the content or academic knowledge to assist their students?" At South Cobb High School, this question is a nonissue as the school provides families with the questions they should ask their students, and families do not need to know the answers—just the right questions to ask. The school is building on the families' strengths, not on any perceived weaknesses. This strategy has worked well as families have become empowered to participate in enhancing the student's success and they can hold their own students accountable for learning while at school.

Data from 2005–2008 support the success of the second-order change. Student attendance increased by 10 percent. When students are in school, they can be taught. With the slogan, "One and done," students increased passing on the GHSGT on the first try; they increased by 2 percent in English and 5 percent in mathematics. Table 8.1 shows the increase in students meeting or exceeding standards from 2005–2008, since Grant became principal. Adding the engagement of families to the learning process is one of the components that Grant believes accelerated the improvement of student achievement.

Table 8.1 South Cobb High School/Georgia High School Graduation Test: English Growth (2005–2008)

Subgroups	Percent Increase in Meeting or Exceeding Standards
All Students	+4.1
Black	+5.4
Hispanic	+6.5
White	+6.4
Students With Disabilities	+15.7
Economically Disadvantaged	+7.1

Charlotte-Mecklenburg Schools: Urban

Students: 134,000   Poverty: 49%

ELL: 13%   ESE Self-Contained: 2%

White: 34%   African American: 42%   Hispanic: 16%

Asian: 4%   American Indian: 4%

LEADER IN ACTION

Peter Gorman, Charlotte-Mecklenburg Schools

> *We are going to close the achievement gap.*
>
> —Peter Gorman

Superintendent Peter Gorman has a history of making changes, and in serving students better than they have been served previously. In our discussion, he shared that Charlotte-Mecklenburg Schools have a 30-percentile difference in achievement between students who live in poverty and those who do not, and between African-American students and non-African-American students. The achievement data related to poverty mirrors the data based on race. His quest is to close the achievement gap.

While reorganization and personnel changes have taken place over a three-year period, Peter seemed excited to share a new strategy to reach families, with the vision of this strategy exponentially affecting the work being done in schools and classrooms each day. This new strategy is "Parent University" and opened in the fall of 2008. Funding comes from private sources and volunteers staff Parent University. His spouse, Sue Gorman, is the "Parent University Champion," or full-time volunteer director. The courses (see www.cms.k12.nc.us/parents/parentuniv) are offered free of charge and address parent needs in four strands: (1) parent awareness, (2) helping your child learn in the twenty-first century, (3) health and wellness, and (4) personal growth. Since this is an outreach strategy, the courses are offered in family-friendly locations throughout the community such as the YMCA, Boys & Girls Clubs, and libraries.

A second excellent example in the Charlotte-Mecklenburg Schools of substantial family engagement in students' learning is "Parent Assistant." Parent Assistant provides online access to each student's individual attendance, assignments, grades, and other pertinent information. Parents and caregivers are provided a password for their students only, so privacy of records is maintained. This type of real-time access to student data is clearly an important trend. It seems that access to information is a twenty-first-century approach to providing parents and caregivers with necessary information for holding their students accountable for doing their part in the learning process.

REFLECTION

Leaders can only control what takes place within the classrooms and generally, within the school day. Engaging families in substantive educative experiences opens the door for educational influence beyond the school day. Technology can be a powerful tool to provide learning opportunities for families, as well as real-time access to students' ongoing school performance. Leveraging the power of the family to support learning is a worthy investment of both dollars and people to improve student achievement.

PRACTICAL TIPS

- Expect personal communication with families, not computer-assisted calls and student take-home newsletters.
- Create family-friendly processes and support for families to engage in student learning.

TRENDS IN ENGAGING FAMILIES IN LEARNING

1. Offering free educative experiences for families at convenient community locations.

2. Providing childcare for family learning experiences.

3. Using technology to provide families with real-time access to student information.

4. Making participation in school personal: calling and inviting each parent/family to participate.

5. Providing each family with a mentor or personal contact.

6. Providing parent guides for each content area or subject.

7. Providing parents with guides for asking their student questions related to benchmarks and standards.

8. Providing interpreters for meetings, and all print in the primary home language of parents.

9. Providing adult English classes and General Equivalency Diploma (GED) classes on the school's campus.

HELPFUL TERMS

General Equivalency Diploma (GED): An alternative for those who do not earn a high school diploma, taking the appropriate course and passing the appropriate exam.

One-way bilingual: Cognitive development in the student's primary home language while developing proficiency in English. The goal is proficiency in both languages and on-grade-level proficiency in content classes.

9

Influence Through the Political Environment

Leaders who are successful with second-order change at both the school and district levels influence through the political environment. They use political processes that include communications vertically and horizontally. This means making negotiations and information transparent, and sometimes public, and always being 100 percent clear on the purpose and desired result in conversations and in leadership strategies. These processes assist when making second-order change because it can be risky and leaders need the support that the political environment, both internally and externally, can provide. As Tim Cool, principal of Cocoa Beach High School shared, "Leaders have to take risks for the betterment of the students." Tim was referring to the risks in making change that may be second-order change for teachers and parents, resulting in the need to communicate clearly with executive leadership such as the superintendent.

Unlike the factors of second-order change (Waters & Marzano, 2007), which served as a basis for interview question 3 for district leaders (see Resource B), school board participation is not cited by anyone as an issue in the implementation. This nonissue probably reflects the sense of urgency superintendents and school boards felt related to making gains in student achievement during the time period of the interviews. As one district administrator said, "Our school board wants us to make change; they expect it."

PRINCIPALS AND THE DISTRICT POLITICAL ENVIRONMENT

In contrast to indicating that support of the school board is not an issue, the political environment of the school district and schools is important (see Resource A, question 4.1). This political environment includes relationships, alliances, coalitions, negotiations, and decision-making processes. While most indicate that they feel great support for the changes they implement and did not direct their comments to the issue, three principals mentioned the district political environment specifically. The first said that she could not have accomplished all that took place without political support and the second said that the political environment does not support second-order change. The latter principal said that the district does not like to talk about student achievement and that the current achievement status is acceptable to those in high-level positions—at least they are not going to create initiatives to bring attention to the lack of student achievement. The third principal mentioned that the leadership style of the district superintendent makes achieving success very difficult, but she was making changes in spite of the superintendent's style.

Another trend in this book that may have political implications is the high faculty, administrator, and staff turnover initially experienced in a number of schools when the second-order changes were introduced and implemented. Leaders should anticipate this possibility and determine, as many of the exemplar principals did, just how they will handle discomfort with the changes. Will they encourage the transfer, or will they not reappoint those who do not positively align themselves with the expectations of the change if it is within the teacher contract? Those who support and supervise principals should expect that this turnover is possible and strategize with the principals on how to address this potential result—knowing that with successful implementation, the faculty, staff, and administrative team will stabilize by about the third year and student achievement will most probably improve.

DISTRICT LEADERS

District leaders, who are not in the superintendent position, nor in line positions supervising and evaluating principals, find the journey to influence student achievement to be less direct. Keep in mind that all of those interviewed worked in districts where there is room for growth in student achievement; no school or district had 100-percent proficiency in reading and mathematics. It appears that the more autonomous the principals are in their decision making—without curricular, instructional, and assessment expectations from their direct line supervisors—the more difficult it is for district staff leaders to influence student achievement, but they can do it through respectful relationships and persistence. District professional developers and curriculum leaders use their relationships to build trust, to provide high-quality professional development and resources, to be service providers, and to use the school's sense of urgency to improve and influence research-based practice. When schools do not feel a sense of urgency, these successful district staff leaders continue on a strategic path to influence those who are receptive to building a critical mass for curricular, instructional, and assessment changes. These changes will in turn influence student achievement. The district leaders in this book are exceptional in their strategies to collaborate and provide support systems to principals who want to change student achievement; simultaneously, they are successful in their strategies to influence those who are receptive.

LEADER IN ACTION

Carol Kelley, New Smyrna Beach High School

> *Give teachers just as much change in expectations as they can handle at one time.*

—Carol Kelley

New Smyrna Beach High School: Small town		
Students: 1,816	Teachers: 123	
Poverty: 20%	ELL: Less than 1%	ESE: 20%
White: 86%	African American: 8%	Hispanic: 2%

Implementing second-order change can be considered risk taking for a principal, since there will likely be some faculty and staff who are uncomfortable with the new expectations. This lack of comfort is a precursor to changing behaviors related to new philosophies and expectations of the daily work in a school.

To be sure that this lack of comfort—and perhaps heightened anxiety—will not derail the intended changes, principals engage in substantive conversations with those who work within the school. According to Carol Kelley, she communicates details and support at the time of need, being careful not to overwhelm teachers or staff with too much change at one time. She wants them to take one step and experience success, and then another and experience success. As Carol mentions, at times, it is difficult for her to personally hold back since she is impatient to make the changes that students need, but it is important to only give the adults what they can handle at a particular time.

Carol also addresses the external political environment. In reorganizing the high school into small learning communities, she meets regularly with her area superintendent and the district superintendent to keep them both informed of the steps being taken. She also updates them on areas of concern or if any red flags are being raised. By keeping the external political players up to date, they are able to provide her with verbal support and guidance, and additional financial resources as well. Through this ongoing external communication, Carol is assured of the advocacy for the changes at the highest level.

As a result of Carol's sensitivity to the political environment that has led to successful second-order changes, the lowest performing quartile of students have made 10 percent reduction in the number of ninth-grade students reading below the proficient level on the Florida Comprehensive Assessment Test (FCAT). More students are participating in Advance Placement (AP) courses and the annual AP test scores are getting better every year.

Wicklow Elementary School: Urban		
Students: 939	Teachers: 70	
Poverty: 63%	ELL: 9%	ESE: 15%
White: 39%	African American: 24%	Hispanic: 25%
Multiracial: 9%	Asian: 3%	

LEADER IN ACTION

Beverly Perrault, Wicklow Elementary School

> *Build trust with open and authentic communication.*
>
> —Beverly Perrault

As an experienced principal, when Beverly Perrault arrived at Wicklow Elementary School in midyear, she had to build trust before implementing any change. Her goal was to develop a trusting relationship with the faculty, staff, and families so that they would be assured that her decisions were driven by what was best for each individual student. She worked to develop trust in the internal political environment to the point that the leadership team began to ask her what changes were needed. She worked with them to develop the changes that were put into place, supported by extensive professional development, alignment of curriculum and instruction, and monitoring assessments.

Beverly also made all data public and transparent. Even when the faculty completed a climate survey, anonymously revealing their likes and dislikes, the results were made public and discussed. This disclosure and openness to feedback surprised the faculty, but it worked in the principal's favor as they saw that the political environment was focused on learning, and that the principal would take risks to be sure that communication was authentic. Each year, student achievement improved and over a five-year period, the school grade awarded by the state moved from a D to an A.

St. Cloud High School: Small town/suburban		
Students: 1,800	Teachers: 112	
Poverty: 38%	ELL: 9%	ESE: 17%
White: 83%	African American: 7%	Hispanic: 10%

LEADER IN ACTION

Pam Tapley, St. Cloud High School

> *The first thing I did was meet with the chamber of commerce to introduce myself and ask for their assistance.*
>
> —Pam Tapley

As a novice principal, Pam Tapley followed a long-time principal. During that time, the local school community changed from one whose main industry was ranching to a more suburban one. However, the historical power structure was still in place in the school, along with the community and state expectations for accountability.

As a savvy political force, Pam immediately met with the town's chamber of commerce to introduce herself and share a vision for the school. The purpose was to engage their support, since her leadership would be a dramatic departure from the previous principal. The school was in desperate need of a facelift both physically and academically, so the chamber's volunteers assisted with the physical renewal—painting, landscaping, and cleaning. When the teachers and students returned to school, the renewal represented respect for them. Pam continues to work closely with the external political environment, participating actively with the chamber and with service organizations. This all serves to ward off questions or concerns that may arise in the community.

Externally, with the district office, Pam was quick to pursue building a new facility. Rebuilding not only includes a contemporary facade, but also the technological infrastructure needed for the students and teachers. Technology was woefully inadequate in 2007, but even in the outdated building, Pam was successful in providing as many up-to-date resources as possible without the new facility.

Along with these changes, one would expect extensive curricular, instructional, and classroom assessment changes. Yes, Pam proceeded rapidly with sharing high expectations for all faculty, staff, and administrators. Each adult is expected to provide each student with whatever is necessary for success. Literacy is being infused throughout the classes and more AP classes are being offered with an attitude of inclusion. As Pam shared, "I care so much about these students that teachers are held accountable. I know this is where I belong." The change in expectations has caused some change in personnel, but many faculty and staff welcomed the positive focus on students and the additional support. Internally, the political environment has taken a positive turn as clear expectations have caused some to leave or retire, but others feel empowered to serve students better.

By working through the internal and external political environment, in a short time, there has been a positive change in student achievement. In 2007–2008, the percent of ninth- and tenth-grade students scoring proficient and above increased in reading, writing, mathematics, and science.

LEADER IN ACTION

Barbara Jenkins, Orange County Public Schools

> *We have to be transparent in our goals, our accomplishments, and our focus on the students.*

—Barbara Jenkins

Orange County Public Schools: Urban

Students: 174,000

Poverty: 58%	ELL: 19%	ESE: 15%
White: 34%	African American: 27%	Hispanic: 31%
Asian: 4%	Multiracial: 3%	

Executive leadership in any school district uses political processes to accomplish organizational goals. Executive leaders communicate and negotiate with other political entities at the local, state, and national levels, as well as with the business community. Examples of leveraging the political environment to improve student achievement are provided by Barbara Jenkins, Chief of Staff in Orange County Public Schools, a diverse urban district of about 174,000 students. Barbara's efforts are both internal to the district and external to the public.

Barbara is concerned about the achievement of students in high-poverty elementary schools. As is typically the case, urban schools where students of poverty attend have a revolving door of teachers. This is due to the challenge of teaching students who arrive at kindergarten behind, and continue to have achievement challenges in each ensuing year. To acknowledge teachers whose students make learning gains and to encourage these teachers to remain for the ensuing year, Barbara wanted to provide financial rewards. The hurdle was the teachers' union. The union president agreed that learning was the priority. He also agreed that these students deserved the best teachers, that teaching in those schools was harder work than in many other schools, and that teachers should be compensated appropriately. The challenge was to reach agreement that only teachers whose students made gain would receive an additional $5,000, rather than all teachers in the schools. With unwavering persistence, Barbara reached agreement on a three-year pilot of the annual bonuses for teachers in high-poverty schools whose students make learning gains. This is a huge political accomplishment, and was achieved by maintaining the focus on what was most important—all students learning.

Externally, Barbara knows that the district should be transparent with the various measures indicating fairness in allocation of resources and expertise. Orange County Public Schools should also be transparent in the accomplishments of each of the schools and departments within the district. To provide transparency, public sharing of data, and accountability for making positive changes, Barbara was instrumental in the creation of the "District Scorecard." The District Scorecard (see www.ocps.net/sb/pages/DistrictScorecard.aspx) provides both data and a business plan on twenty-five key measures. By being public, transparent, and accountable, the political environment is open and encourages more dialogue to improve equity and excellence for all students throughout the large district.

REFLECTION

Over the time of interviewing and observing in schools and districts, it has become very clear that when the superintendent identifies a goal or project as the priority, it gets the organizational support, personnel support, financial and resource support, and perhaps even evaluation/research/ monitoring support. Superintendent focus accelerates the implementation of change and perhaps creates a sense of urgency for other leaders within the district and school to take action. In fact, it is common for the focus of the superintendent to show up on principals' evaluations. For instance, one principal shared that his school had been designated a B by the Department of Education and on his annual evaluation it was written, "A school grade of B is unacceptable," creating a sense of urgency to find solutions and to earn an A the following year. Examples of the results of a superintendent's priority include the work of Superintendent Vogel in Chapter 5, Tom Curry in Chapter 6, Anna Marie Cote in Chapter 7, and Superintendent Gorman in Chapter 8. Further review shows that clear focus on all students learning garners political support. Additionally, Table 9.1 shows examples of both external and internal political environments to be considered when implementing second-order change. Transparency, public reporting, and accountability for results positively promote a positive political environment for schools, both internally and externally.

Table 9.1 External and Internal Political Environment: Examples

External Political Environment	Internal Political Environment
Chamber of Commerce	Faculty, Staff, and Administrators
Service Clubs (Rotary, Retired Educators)	Students
Local, State, National Government and Elected Officials: Department of Education	Teachers' Union
Local, State, and National Professional Organizations	Families
Graduates	School and District Foundations
District Administrator (for school-based administrators)	School Board
News Media	Internal Communications
Other Schools and School Districts	Departments and Teams Within the Schools/Districts

PRACTICAL TIPS

- Map out the coalitions within and outside of the school.
- Strategize to communicate priorities and target changes with coalitions.

TRENDS IN LEVERAGING THE POLITICAL ENVIRONMENT

1. Building trust and respectful relationships to support needed change for learning internally and externally.

2. Clarity about the purpose and desired result of the negotiations.

3. Being transparent and public, providing accurate data.

4. Aligning priorities across all levels of the organization.

5. Tolerance of discomfort with changes for leading, teaching, and learning.

6. Maintaining accurate communications with leaders at the highest level and not understating problems or successes.

7. Creating a political environment that is supportive of change to improve learning.

HELPFUL TERMS

External political environment: Those outside of the immediate setting: community, district for school-based leaders.

Internal political environment: Those within the immediate setting: faculty, administrators, staff within a school.

Line supervisor: Has direct responsibility for principal performance, evaluates principals.

Staff supervisor: Supports leadership with no supervisory responsibility of principals.

Transparent: Authentic and accurate data and communication.

10

Reflections on Leading Learning for Second-Order Change

Principals and district leaders indicate that the implementation of second-order change is really hard, that they work many hours—maybe up to fifteen hours a day—during the implementation. After implementation, success becomes the norm and the intensity seems to ease up a little; perhaps because faculty are aligned. However, they continue to work long hours and work at continuous improvement of learning. Successful implementation does not mean institutionalization of change since enough time may not have passed to determine if that is the case. Furthermore, as more educational research emerges, these leaders are aware that new research-based changes will continue to take place. However, with the change in culture noted by every leader, there will be an expectation of institutionalization of a culture focused on learning, with continued change and improvements. Additionally, once teachers experience the type of self-efficacy and empowerment that these leader actions create, even when faced with difficult decisions such as deep budget cuts, teachers collaborate to maintain the positive changes already in place.

Most of the examples in this text reflect the changing student demographics. Many of the schools or districts categorized as suburban have high poverty rates and perhaps high English-language-learner populations, or high special-education populations. Yet, diversity is growing among districts and schools regardless of their locations, requiring successful school leaders to examine the curricular, instructional, and assessment-related elements of their schools.

While the leader action themes provide insight into leadership for second-order change, readers may be interested in specific elements of the changes related to curriculum, instruction, instructional resources, student work, and assessment concepts, which when implemented, result in positive gains in student achievement. Following are instructional and curricular elements that may provide further guidance. There is no particular program or singular innovation that is consistent in each of the schools and districts. What is important is the horizontal and vertical alignment of curriculum, instruction, student work, and assessment (Taylor & Gunter, 2006; Taylor, 2007) and using the leader action themes to do so. Table 1.3 shows these nine themes, focusing the culture on learning in the center and the first circle containing the eight others. The typical elements of the second-order changes appear in the outer band.

Many of the examples in this book illustrate changes in expectations for reading, writing, thinking, and mathematics. This is not to say that innovations in other content areas are not important. But in most states, these are the curriculum areas where schools and districts are held directly accountable. Also, success in science, social studies, and other content areas is often dependent upon the improvement of students in the processes of reading (vocabulary, fluency, comprehension); higher-level thinking (application, synthesis, analysis, evaluation); and writing with content texts, particularly at the middle and high school levels. As Larry Gerardot, principal of Anthis Career Center in Indiana, reflected, "I am anxious for us to reach the tipping point in literacy." While his teachers are career and technical-content experts, he works diligently with them to become pedagogy experts, particularly with research-based literacy infusion to improve the student's vocabulary, fluency, speaking, thinking, and comprehension.

CURRICULUM

Consistently, curriculum is aligned both vertically (grade to grade) and horizontally (across teachers within the grade). This means that an observer in several third-grade classrooms will see similar concepts addressed, resources used, and student work accomplished. Learning centers will be the same and are probably planned for together by the grade-level teachers, perhaps with the support of a literacy or instructional coach. The same concept applies to high school content classrooms; world history or algebra would be the same regardless of the teacher or period taught or grouping of students within the classes. What is most critical for gains in student achievement is that this aligned curriculum represents standards based on grade-level curriculum regardless of the demographic characteristics of the students. Rigor is essential; if the teachers align vertically and horizontally at a low level, then the students will not grow academically.

The order of the curriculum, and time spent with particular skills and concepts, reflects the formal accountability of the assessment schedule. Curriculum standards which are highly measured or essential are taught earlier in the school year. Curriculum standards which are not measured (nice to know, but not measured or already mastered) are addressed after the formal assessment.

Curriculum is enhanced for all achievement levels of students—those performing below grade level, at grade level, and above grade level. Interventions in reading and mathematics are implemented for those performing below grade level. Particular attention is paid to fluency in reading and fluency with mathematical concepts such as addition, subtraction, multiplication, and division. Intervention means more time, more scaffolding, more intense instruction, different resources, and most probably technology to accelerate learning so that students can close the achievement gap. Monitoring interventions for fidelity to the research-based model is a consideration, since only with fidelity will the results of interventions be maximized.

An attitude of inclusion into higher-level classes, such as honors or Advanced Placement, is present. These schools encourage students to aspire to higher achievement and to expose themselves to more difficult curriculum with the expectation of research-based instruction to ensure success. The school leaders take monitoring students' success in such classes seriously. A characteristic of schools making gains with these classes is the teachers' positive attitudes toward inclusion and better understanding of how to assist each student to be successful, rather than selecting students guaranteed to be successful independently.

INSTRUCTION

Contemporary research guides instruction in all grade levels, from prekindergarten through twelfth grades. This includes all content areas: reading, language arts, mathematics, science, social students, foreign language, domestic arts, art, humanities, music, technology, and career education. Teachers engage students in whole class, small groups, pairs, and individually. Teachers are not at their desks, at their computers, nor sitting on a stool in front of the class. Rather, they move around the classroom providing scaffolding and support, checking for accuracy and understanding, and giving students individual instruction, clarifications, and correctives. Scaffolding means that the level of support is related to difficulty of the concept or text, and the ability of the students to read or understand it independently. Therefore, high support is provided early, and then tapers off as students develop independent expertise, skill, and knowledge.

Research-based vocabulary instruction is implemented across all classes. Lists of words to look up in dictionaries are not the typical practice. Instead, to create mental models and help make connections to previous learning, words are presented with student definitions and visuals. Emphasis is on content vocabulary at grade level in speaking, reading, and writing.

Comprehension strategies are taught, modeled, and practiced across all grade levels and content areas. Strategies are used to check for understanding before reading, during reading, and after reading. Some of the most common and effective comprehension strategies are summarization, prediction, clarification, connections, evaluation, and question asking (Taylor, 2007).

Students read content passages or are introduced to a mathematics concept and are then scaffolded to higher levels of comprehension. Teachers begin with high support, model, provide guided practice, and then move to independent practice. The degree of support is dependent upon the level of difficulty of the text or work and the ability of the student to independently access it successfully. It is important to note that teachers do not assign independent practice until students demonstrate success. This includes mathematics problems and homework. Homework is independent practice and reserved to practice skills and concepts already learned. It is never for introduction of a concept, passage, or skill. Individual assessment takes place after success in independent practice. Table 10.1 illustrates the concept of scaffolding instruction.

Writing is infused and expected in all classes. Writing is a high-level cognitive process and is to be used for students to show what they know. Writing should be used before, during, and after instruction and reading. Short writing, such as a one-sentence summary of a section or two things to remember, helps students to comprehend and provides the teacher quick checks on understanding. Graphic organizers can assist students in creating a concrete understanding of abstract concepts, using writing to show the understanding. Writing using academic language across all content areas, particularly nonfiction writing, results in gains in student achievement in reading.

Most schools visited encourage teachers to ask questions on higher levels and to include high-level thinking in their instruction. In my own consultations, I find that many schools have a preponderance of low-level comprehension work and questions for students. Improving student achievement on formal assessments requires students to respond to items that require higher levels of thinking—application, synthesis, analysis, evaluation, and creation of new knowledge (Taylor, 2007).

Students who find work to be more difficult are provided background information necessary for success in the given content. This does not mean

Table 10.1 Scaffolding Instruction for Student Success

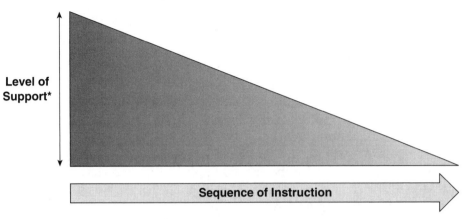

Level of Support*

Sequence of Instruction

Introduction:	Guided Practice:	Independent Practice:	Assessment:
Direct instruction	Pairs, small groups	Individual work	Feedback
Background knowledge	Cooperative learning	Check fluency	Correctives
Modeling	Understanding checks	Check accuracy	Independence
Vocabulary	Accuracy checks	Clarifications	
Mental model	Experiential	Correctives	
Visuals	Clarifications	Reflection	
Demonstration	Correctives	Self-assessment	

The level of support depends upon the difficulty of the text/concepts and the ability of the learner to comprehend the text/concepts independently.

to preteach, but to provide background information, such as vocabulary or conceptual knowledge, that the students are expected to know and must know to easily learn the new content.

In schools making gains in student achievement, evidence indicates that student assignments are on grade level. Entertaining assignments (coloring, cutting, and pasting) are not seen during designated content-learning time. If present, these types of experiences take place in nonacademic time, such as recess. I witnessed a nonexample of this during my previous research, when I saw students not focused on grade-level content. While visiting an elementary school, I observed students in each grade level coloring the same pumpkin handout right before Halloween. Even if coloring the pumpkin orange was instructionally appropriate for kindergarten or first grade, it certainly was not appropriate for the upper grades and not year after year. It was no surprise that this school did not make significant gains in student achievement until the leadership changed! The practice of monitoring on grade-level work and minimizing nonacademic experiences maximizes learning time.

ASSESSMENT

In schools making gains, there is evidence that summative assessment is expected to be on grade level after the teacher carefully scaffolds the students to independent work. A number of the leaders in this text, at all grade levels, indicate that teachers are developing common assessments through collaboration with the expectation of increasing rigor. Continuous checks for understanding guides the teachers to provide clarifications, additional learning opportunities, or to move ahead in the curriculum. Leaders strategize to find more learning time before and after the school day, within the school day (such as during lunch), on weekends, and during break time between school terms.

Leaders ensure that monitoring assessments are ongoing in at least reading and mathematics. As noted in Chapter 7, leaders and teachers study data continuously and use the data to guide instruction. The relationship between ongoing monitoring assessments and the formal accountability assessments are known and used to predict gains in student achievement.

CONCLUDING THOUGHTS

When superintendents, district leaders, and school-based leaders align priorities, student achievement improves fairly quickly. While there are no consistent academic resources, there are common priorities which typically focus on improving reading and writing for all students at all grade levels. This alignment is the best possible scenario for implementation of second-order change. Successful leaders in implementing second-order change share incorporation of at least eight of the nine leader action themes represented in this book. Their change leadership is complex but strategic and replicable. While each context is different, the leaders are consistent in their own behaviors and commitments to all students learning more. None of them make excuses for the students, faculty, staff, or themselves. In contrast, they are purposeful and deliberate in their actions, and grounded in sound research and practice. The result is schools and districts where more students learn more often.

In thinking about your second-order change leadership, and with Table 10.2 as a guide, reflect on the leader action themes and elements of the changes in your own strategizing for success.

Table 10.2 Checklist for Implementation of Second-Order Change

Leader Action Theme	Examples	Guiding Questions	What I will do or have done . . .
Focus the culture of the school on learning.	Demonstrate high expectations for all students.	Are all students expected to meet on-grade-level standards? How does student work represent rigor for all students? How do you ensure that diverse students are invited to enroll in advanced, honors, AP classes?	
Make decisions for student learning.	Organize all resources to maximize effectiveness of student learning (personnel, time, space, resources).	How do resource decisions maximize achievement of all students? How do you ensure that all adults maximize student-learning time? How do the organizational structures facilitate learning?	
Stimulate intellectual growth.	Develop targeted expertise. Target professional development. Lead and participate with faculty. Evolve to collegial coaching.	To what extent are you conversant about the research that guides your leadership? How are you becoming an expert in content/skills, and concepts for which you expect teacher expertise?	
Invest in the change.	Delegate other items. Personally lead the change.	Where and how do you spend the majority of your time?	
Expect collaboration and results from collaboration.	Expect, model, and participate in collaboration. Plan for implementation and accountability.	How do you model the value of collaboration for yourself/others? What accountability is in place for collaboration?	

(Continued)

Table 10.2 (Continued)

Leader Action Theme	Examples	Guiding Questions	What I will do or have done . . . .
Strategize for consistency.	Speak with one voice. Create a system for communication and feedback.	Do you share the strategy? Is there a visual to show others your system?	
Expect data-based decision making at the student level.	Provide time, resources, and expectation of ongoing use of data to inform instruction. Adopt a data-management system that is easy to use.	What types of data are available for real-time access? To what extent is real-time data, including classroom data, used to make instructional decisions?	
Engage families in learning.	Provide families with real-time data that is easy to access. Make personal connections.	To what extent do you and adults in your school personally communicate with families? How easy is it to access up-to-date student data, including classroom data for families?	
Influence through the political environment.	Maintain close communication with superiors and subordinates regarding expectations and anticipated challenges. Leverage relationships externally and internally.	How do you strategically communicate with executive leadership related to successes and potential issues? To what extent are internal and external communications authentic?	

Leader Action Theme	Examples	Guiding Questions	What I will do or have done . . .
Attend to the elements of change that influence student achievement for students who lack proficiency, are proficient, or exceed proficient standards.	Align vertically and horizontally on-grade-level curriculum, instruction, assessment, student work, and resources. Infuse research-based literacy (reading, writing, speaking, thinking). Implement mathematics intervention and research-based instruction. Infuse technology. Scaffold learning. Implement research-based interventions, accelerations, etc.	Is the curriculum aligned horizontally and vertically? To what extent is student work studied to determine rigor for each grade and course? To what extent is literacy infused throughout the school? To what extent are intensive interventions (mathematics, literacy) implemented and monitored? To what extent is technology infusion evident? How do you know that teachers scaffold students to success?	

Resource A

Principal Interview Protocol

Purpose: The purpose of the research is to determine to what extent principals who have led successful second-order change have done so aligned with the research on leading change. This research is not to evaluate the innovation, or the effectiveness, in any way. The innovations discussed and leaders interviewed have been selected because of their documented success and recommendations from experts in the field.

Research Questions

1. To what extent do principals who have led successful second-order change exhibit the seven factors related to successful second-order change identified by Marzano, Waters, and McNulty (2005)?

2. To what extent do principals who have led successful second-order change create structures and systems to support the change?

3. What themes, conclusions, or questions related to leadership for second-order change have not been previously identified but emerge in interviews?

Directions

Before the interview: Collect available data and information related to interview items and so indicate on the interview protocol.

During the interview: Ask for the description of the innovation and evidence of success of the innovation in Section I. Listen for items in Sections II and III for which you did not gather evidence before the interview. If items are neither answered with data nor evidence gathered before the interview nor in Section I, with political sensitivity, probe for this information, being respectful of the interviewee's time. If you have evidence of any of the items from other sources, do not ask for it.

After the interview: Review data, evidence, and interview responses to determine new themes or conclusions that may be drawn from the investigation or questions that emerged regarding second-order change, and note in Section IV.

Second-Order Change Study
Principal Interview Protocol

Interviewee: Position:

Innovation: Interview date:

Interviewer:

Section I. Innovation

1. Describe the innovation and the role you played in the design, implementation, and evaluation.

2. How do you know it was successful? Data? Evidence?

Section II. Factors of Second-Order Change

1. Knowledge of Curriculum, Instruction, and Assessment.

"Knowing how the innovation will affect these and provide conceptual guidance in these areas" (Marzano, Waters, & McNulty, 2005, p. 70).

1. How did the innovation affect curriculum?

2. How did the innovation affect instruction?

3. How did the innovation affect assessment?

4. Give an example of your work individually or in groups regarding the innovation.

(Marzano et al., 2005)

2. Optimizer.

"Being the driving force behind the innovation and fostering the belief that it can produce exceptional results if members are willing to apply themselves" (Marzano et al., p. 72).

1. Who provided the most leadership for implementation of the innovation?

2. What role did you play in implementing the innovation?

3. Can you give an example of speaking positively about it, and provide examples of other schools being successful?

4. How did you instill confidence in others that this innovation would yield results?

5. Provide examples of you voicing continued confidence in the innovation's success and impact.

6. How were roadblocks and challenges identified and addressed?

(Marzano et al., 2005)

3. Intellectual Stimulation.

"Being knowledgeable about the research and theory regarding the innovation and fostering the knowledge among staff through reading and discussion" (Marzano et al., p. 72).

1. Can you tell me about the research or theoretical background of the innovation?

2. How did professional staff learn about the theory and research behind it?

3. Give an example of you including it in conversations, leading discussions, or asking questions.

(Marzano et al., 2005)

4. Change Agent.

"Challenging the status quo and being willing to move forward on the innovation without a guarantee of success" (Marzano et al., p. 72).

1. What political processes were used to move the innovation beyond the status quo?

2. Give an example of you raising issues related to student achievement.

3. Give an example of you sharing data.

4. Give an example of you providing comparisons of where the school/district was and where it needs to be.

5. Can you think of a time when you demonstrated tolerance for ambiguity related to the innovation?

(Marzano et al., 2005)

5. Monitoring/Evaluating.

"*Continually monitoring the impact of the innovation*" (Marzano et al., p. 72).

1. What type of monitoring of results has taken place? Formative? Summative?

2. What other monitoring or evaluations are planned?

3. Can you think of a time when you conducted walkthroughs or visits?

(Marzano et al., 2005)

6. Flexibility.

"*Being both directive and nondirective relative to the innovation as the situation warrants*" (Marzano et al., p. 72).

1. Provide an example of you being flexible during the design, implementation, or evaluation of the innovation.

2. Provide an example of adjusting plans as needed.

3. What protocols for evaluation were used or did discussions bog down?

(Marzano et al., 2005)

7. Ideals/Beliefs.

"*Operating in a manner consistent with his ideas and beliefs relative to the innovation*" (Marzano et al., p. 72).

1. How was consistency in leadership related to the innovation obtained?

2. What role did you play in achieving consistency?

3. How did you communicate regarding the innovation?

4. What are examples of strategic questions that you asked when actions were not aligned with the core beliefs/expectations?

(Marzano et al., 2005)

Section III. Organizational Decisions to Create New Systems

Implementing structures, reorganization, reporting, personal positions, instructional resources, and purchased services (Bolman & Deal, 2003; Taylor & Collins, 2003).

1. What structural changes were made?

2. Were any positions added or reassigned?

3. What professional development was purchased, funded, or organized?

4. What instructional resources or technology solutions were implemented?

5. Were partnerships established with partners outside of the school/district for mutual benefit?

Section IV. Interviewer's Conclusions, New Themes, or Questions Related to Second-Order Change

Resource B

District Leader Interview Protocol

Interviewee: Position: Time in position:

Innovation: Interview date:

Interviewer:

Purpose: The purpose of the research is to determine to what extent district leaders who have led successful second-order change have done so aligned with the research on leading change. This research is not to evaluate the innovation, or the effectiveness, in any way. The innovations discussed and leaders interviewed have been selected because of their documented success and recommendations from experts in the field.

Research Questions

1. To what extent do district leaders who have led successful second-order change exhibit the six factors related to successful second-order change identified by Waters and Marzano (2007)?

2. To what extent do district leaders who have led successful second-order change create structures and systems to support the change?

3. What themes, conclusions, or questions related to leadership for second-order change have not been previously identified but emerge in interviews?

4. To what extent does longevity in the superintendent position relate to successful change?

Directions

Before the interview: Collect available data and information related to interview items and so indicate on the interview protocol.

During the interview: Ask for the description of the innovation and evidence of success of the innovation in Section I. Listen for items in Sections II and III for which you did not gather evidence before the interview. If items are neither answered with data or evidence gathered before the interview nor in Section I, with political sensitivity, probe for this information, being respectful of the interviewee's time. If you have evidence of any of the items from other sources, do not ask for it.

After the interview: Review data, evidence, and interview responses to determine new themes or conclusions that may be drawn from the investigation or questions that emerged regarding second-order change and note in Section IV.

District Leader Interview Protocol

Interviewee: Position:

Innovation: Interview date:

Interviewer:

Section I. Innovation

1. Describe the innovation and the role you played in the design, implementation, and evaluation.

2. How do you know it was successful? What was the average student gain in student achievement? Data? Evidence?

Section II. Factors of Second-Order Change

1. Goal-Setting Process.

1. Share the goal-setting process in curriculum and in instruction.

2. To what extent are goals focused on change, rather than status quo?

3. How were goals shared with district administrators and teachers, and with the schools?

2. Nonnegotiable Goals for Achievement and Instruction.

1. How did you model understanding of instructional design?

2. Which schools enacted these agreed-upon goals?

3. To what extent were school-based action plans designed around these goals?

4. Is there a common framework for instruction or is it determined at the school level (instructional language, vocabulary, design)? How are instructional strategies determined to address varied needs?

5. Provide examples of how principals support the goals explicitly and implicitly. Were there examples of principals subverting the goals?

3. Board Alignment With and Support for the Goals.

1. How did the board demonstrate support for the goals?

2. How did the board maintain these goals as top priority and keep other competing priorities from subverting them?

3. What professional development was provided for the board related to the goals? How did you determine the effectiveness of the professional development?

4. How did you and the board remain politically and situationally aware of the climate regarding the goals?

4. Monitoring Achievement and Instructional Goals.

1. Provide examples of how you monitored achievement and progress toward goal attainment. Was there an evaluation program?

2. How did you ensure that each school monitors its progress?

3. When discrepancies in teacher instruction and the curricular and instructional expectations exist, what happens?

4. How often do you observe classrooms?

5. Describe the system used to implement the change.

6. How were efforts among individuals and groups coordinated so that response to needs and failures could be made?

5. Use of Resources to Support the Goals for Instruction and Achievement.

1. How were resources (time, money, people, materials) reallocated to ensure success?

2. How were professional development resources reallocated both at the district and school level? Teachers and administrators? Was there a master plan?

3. Describe the instructional and resource management system supporting the implementation.

6. Defined Autonomy and Superintendent Relationship With Schools.

1. To what extent do principals have a definition of their autonomy?

2. To what extent do school principals have autonomy to determine goals?

3. To what extent do school principals have autonomy to determine how to reach the goals?

4. To what extent are principals expected to adopt the district goals for curriculum and instruction?

5. How does teacher evaluation relate to principal priorities?

6. How do you know that principals speak with teachers about results?

7. How do you know that the school implements practices focused on all students being successful?

8. Give an example of you demonstrating the expectation that principals are instructional leaders.

9. Give an example of you promoting the innovation.

Section III. Organizational Decisions to Create New Systems

Implementing structures, reorganization, reporting, personal positions, instructional resources, and purchased services (Taylor & Collins, 2003; Bolman & Deal, 2003).

1. What structural changes were made?

2. Were any positions added or reassigned?

3. What professional development was purchased, funded, or organized?

4. What instructional resources or technology solutions were implemented?

5. Were partnerships established with partners outside of the school/district for mutual benefit?

Section IV. Interviewer's Conclusions, New Themes, or Questions Related to Second-Order Change

Resource C

Guidelines for Collaborative Sessions,
Rimfire Elementary School

Agreements

- ✓ Listen with an open mind.
- ✓ Focus on the information, not the person.
- ✓ Ask for specific feedback.
- ✓ Do not become defensive.
- ✓ Be honest.
- ✓ Express appreciation.

Stems for Giving Feedback

- ✓ I like the way . . .
- ✓ It is evident that . . .
- ✓ I wonder if you thought . . .
- ✓ Did you consider . . .
- ✓ Could you explain/clarify . . .
- ✓ I would like to know more about . . .

Resource D

Team Meeting Notes, Hunter's Creek Middle School

Team:	**Date:**
Members present:	

General School Information:

Team leaders:

Important dates:

Instructional Practices:

Strategies used for progress toward school-improvement goals:

FCAT questions and strategies:

Extended-thinking/higher-order activities:

Reading strategies:

Student Data Discussed (i.e., FCAT, C-BAT, academics, attendance, behavior, affective):

Parent contact results:

Follow-Up Activities:

Resource E

Leadership Team, Crystal River High School (2007–2008)

	Name	Leadership Role	Responsibility
Lead Teachers of WOW/ PDP- Core Academic Leaders	Teacher A	Foreign Language, Language Arts, Fine Arts, Reading Department Head	• Facilitate leadership of school academic departments. • Coordinate WOW process. • Lead budget process.
	Teacher B	Social Studies, Health Academy, PE, NJROTC Department Head	
	Teacher C	Math, Science, Media, Technology Department Head	
	Teacher D	Vocational, ESE Department Head	
Lead Teachers of Progress Monitoring	Teacher E	Freshman Academy Leader, Ninth-Grade Progress Monitoring Leader	• Coordinate data and facilitate monthly progress-monitoring meeting for students who are at risk. • Assist with leading departments.
	Teacher F	Eleventh-Grade Progress Monitoring Team Leader, Science Department Head	

	Name	Leadership Role	Responsibility
	Teacher G	Health Academy Team Leader, Tenth-Grade Progress Monitoring Leader	• Attend monthly team leader meetings. • Facilitate budgets.
	Teacher H	Twelfth-Grade Progress Monitoring Leader (Graduation Rate and Dropout)	
Lead Teachers of Professional Development and Professional Study Groups	Teacher I	ROTC and PE Department Head	• Facilitate bimonthly staff development sessions, also lead professional study groups. • Facilitate students and staff with SRI/MAZE/FORF testing. • Assist staff with data summary connecting to PDP.
	Teacher J	Business/Business Academy	
	Teacher K	English Department Head	
	Teacher L	Transition Math Department Head	

Note: Team also includes the lead guidance counselor with three school counselors.

Resource F

Walkthrough Comment Card, Citrus County Schools

Side 1

DATE/TIME	OBSERVER	GR/SUBJ	COMMENTS	STANDARD

Standard 1: The teacher supports the beliefs, shared vision, and mission adopted by the district.

Standard 2: The teacher designs knowledge work containing student-focused qualities that reflect the needs of the students, parents, school system, and community: content and substance, organization of knowledge, product focus, clear and compelling standards, choice, protection from adverse consequences, affirmation of performance, opportunities for affiliation, novelty and variety, authenticity.

Standard 3: The teacher manages the resources of time, people, space, information, and technology in order to enhance the qualities of the work provided to students.

Standard 4: The teacher continuously monitors the extent to which students are engaging in the work, persisting with the work, and experiencing satisfaction in the products of the work; teacher modifies the work accordingly.

Standard 5: The teacher demonstrates leadership.

Side 2

Essential Questions:	Vocabulary:	Higher-Order Thinking:
☐ Posted ☐ Guided instruction ☐ Used to measure learning	☐ Posted word walls, print-rich classroom ☐ Root words/base words or other vocabulary instruction ☐ Integrated into learning	☐ Higher-level questions ☐ Instruction reflected critical thinking ☐ Engaging activity reflected higher-order thinking
Reading Comprehension:	**Data-Driven Instruction:**	**Reading/Writing Connection:**
☐ Reading comprehension strategies guide reading instruction ☐ Comprehension questions	☐ Profile data sheets maintained in plan book ☐ Accomodations made to instruction based on data	☐ Writing processes posted ☐ Rubrics, graphic organizers used ☐ Samples of student writing

Reading and Writing Strategies:

Prediction ☐	Visualization ☐	Connections ☐
Questioning ☐	Clarification ☐	Evaluation ☐
Summarization ☐	Use of Graphic Organizers ☐	

Resource G

Ridgeback Reflections,
Central Ridge Elementary School

Ridgeback Reflections

September 12, 2008

Essential Question = What benefits are you seeing in using an essential question?

From Kerri Cark's perspective . . . I view essential questions as a way to introduce the lesson and stay focused throughout the lesson.

Cathy Farrell has these thoughts. . . .

The benefit I'm seeing by using the essential question is that my lesson is more focused on what I want to get across to the students. I use it as a blueprint to organize my lesson and it helps me keep the extraneous threads out of my lessons. I also use it as the introduction to my lesson and the review. If the students can't answer the question at the wrap-up,

then I'm not clear in my delivery and I need to revisit it again by presenting it in a different way.

Resource H

Excerpts From Attendance Policy,
Leesburg High School

1. Excused absences include: medical, court appearances, death in the family, or unusual circumstances. Absences shall be documented with a doctor's note, court notice, or other authorized documentation to excuse the absence.
   - Three parent notes per eighteen-week term will be accepted to excuse absences.
   - All other absences will be counted as unexcused.
   - More than three excused absences will be considered excessive, therefore a note from a licensed physician will be required to excuse the absence.
   - After two and before four unexcused absences, a school authority will notify the parent or guardian.
   - Once a student has four or more unexcused absences, the maximum grade of 59 will be given for each course concerned.

2. Incentives for Good Attendance.
   - Zero days absent = 9 points added to exam
   - One day absent = 6 points added to exam
   - Two–three days absent = 3 points added to exam

3. Disincentive for Excessive Absences.
   - Four unexcused absences will result in a failing grade (59) for that semester in each course concerned. Exams can still be taken for full credit so students may still pass with an acceptable exam grade.

References

Allen, J. (2008). Family partnerships that count. *Educational Leadership, 66* (1), 22–27.

Blase, J., & Blase, J. (2001). *Empowering teachers* (2nd ed.). Thousand Oaks, CA: Corwin.

Blase, J., & Blase, J. (2004). *Handbook of instructional leadership* (2nd ed.). Thousand Oaks, CA: Corwin.

Bolman, L., & Deal, T. E. (2003). *Reframing organizations.* San Francisco: Wiley.

Dufour, R. (2004). What is a professional learning community? *Educational Leadership, 61* (8), 6–11.

Dufour, R., & Eaker, R. (1998). *Professional learning communities at work: Best practices for enhancing student achievement.* Alexandria, VA: Association for Supervision and Curriculum Development.

Eaker, R., Dufour, R., & Dufour, R. (2002). *Getting started: Reculturing schools to become professional learning communities.* Bloomington, IN: National Educational Service.

Fullan, M. (2006). *Turnaround leadership.* San Francisco: Wiley.

Glickman, C. D. (2002). *Leadership for learning: How to help teachers succeed.* Alexandria, VA: Association for Supervision and Curriculum Development.

Henderson, A. T., & Mapp, K. L. (2002). *A new wave of evidence: The impact of school, family and community connections on student achievement.* Austin, TX: National Center for Family & Community Connections With Schools.

Honig, M. I., & Hatch, T. C. (2004). Crafting coherence: How schools strategically manage multiple, external demands. *Educational Researcher, 33* (8), 16–30.

Katzenbach, J. R., & Smith, D. K. (1993). *The wisdom of teams: Creating the high-performance organization.* Boston: Harvard Business School Press.

Lee, J., Grigg, W., & Donahue, P. (2007). *The nation's report card: Reading 2007.* Washington, DC: National Center for Education Statistics, Institute of Education Sciences, U.S. Department of Education.

Leithwood, K., Louis, K. S., Anderson, S., & Wahlstrom, K. (2004). *How leadership Influences student learning: Executive summary.* New York: Wallace Foundation. Retrieved September 20, 2008, from www.wallacefoundation.org/KnowledgeCenter/KnowledgeTopics/EducationLeadership/Documents/HowLeadershipInfluencesStudentLearningES.htm

Little, J. W. (1993). Teachers professional development in a climate of educational reform. *Educational Evaluation and Policy Analysis, 15* (2), 129–152.

Marzano, R. J. (2003). *What works in schools: Translating research into action.* Alexandria, VA: Association for Supervision and Curriculum Development.

Marzano, R. J. (2004*). Building background knowledge.* Alexandria, VA: Association for Supervision and Curriculum Development.

Marzano, R. J., & Pickering, D. J. (2005). *Building academic vocabulary.* Alexandria, VA: Association for Supervision and Curriculum Development.

Marzano, R. J., Waters, T., & McNulty, B. A. (2005). *School leadership that works.* Alexandria, VA: Association for Supervision and Curriculum Development.

Moxley, D. E., & Taylor, R. T. (2006). *Literacy coaching: A handbook for school leaders.* Thousand Oaks, CA: Corwin and National Association of Secondary School Principals.

Newman, F., Smith, B., Allensworth, E., & Bryk, A. (2001). Instructional program coherence: What it is and why it should guide school improvement policy. *Educational Evaluation and Policy Analysis, 23* (4), 297–321.

Peterson, K. D. (2002). Positive or negative. *Journal of Staff Development, 23* (3), 10–15.

Peterson, K. D., & Deal, T. E. (2002). *The shaping school culture fieldbook.* San Francisco: Jossey-Bass.

Reeves, D. B. (2004). *Accountability for learning: How teachers and school leaders can take charge.* Alexandria, VA: Association for Supervision and Curriculum Development.

Reeves, D. B. (2006). *The learning leader: How to focus school improvement for better results.* Alexandria, VA: Association for Supervision and Curriculum Development.

Reeves, D. B. (Ed.). (2008a). *Ahead of the curve: The power of assessment to transform teaching and learning.* Bloomington, IN: Solution Tree.

Reeves, D. B. (2008b). *Reframing teacher leadership to improve your school.* Alexandria, VA: Association for Supervision and Curriculum Development.

Schmoker, M. (2006). *Results now: How we can achieve unprecedented achievements in teaching and learning.* Alexandria, VA: Association for Supervision and Curriculum Development.

Taylor, R. T. (2007). *Improving reading, writing, and content learning for students in Grades 4–12.* Thousand Oaks, CA: Corwin.

Taylor, R. T., & Chanter, C. (2008). Systematically making reading the center of high school. *The AASA Journal of Scholarship and Practice, 5* (3), 37–45.

Taylor, R. T., & Collins, V. D. (2003). *Literacy leadership for Grades 5–12.* Alexandria, VA: Association for Supervision and Curriculum Development.

Taylor, R. T., & Gunter, G. A. (2006). *The K–12 literacy leadership fieldbook.* Thousand Oaks, CA: Corwin.

Taylor, R. T., & Moxley, D. E. (2008). Leadership for literacy coaching: Evolving research. *ERS Spectrum, 26* (3), 1–6.

Wagner, T., & Kagan, R. (2006). *Change leadership.* San Francisco: Wiley.

Waters, T. J., & Marzano, R. J. (2007). School district leadership that works: The effect of superintendent leadership on student achievement. *ERS Spectrum, 25* (2), 1–12.

Index

CORWIN

A SAGE Company

The Corwin logo—a raven striding across an open book—represents the union of courage and learning. Corwin is committed to improving education for all learners by publishing books and other professional development resources for those serving the field of PreK–12 education. By providing practical, hands-on materials, Corwin continues to carry out the promise of its motto: **"Helping Educators Do Their Work Better."**